# JIMMY SWAGGART: TO OBEY GOD RATHER THAN MEN

# JIMMY SWAGGART: TO OBEY GOD RATHER THAN MEN

by

Charles R. Fontaine
Lynda K. Fontaine

The Kerusso Company, Inc.
P.O. Box 1168
Crockett, Texas  75835-1168

Special thanks to

Jack L. Worth
and
Mary C. Worth

for their unwavering love and support


and to

Jay L. Fontaine

for his excellent research assistance

# CONTENTS

## SECTON THREE – THE FINANCIAL SUPPORT FOR JIMMY SWAGGART MINISTRIES

## SECTION FOUR – A POTPOURRI

# FOREWORD

Occasionally a book comes along that "blows my doors off." *Jimmy Swaggart: To Obey God Rather Than Men* has affected me in that way.

Charles Fontaine was an electronic technician for many years. He is not a preacher, teacher, or theologian. Vocationally, he is the custodian at a local independent church in Hot Springs, Arkansas. He also works in maintenance at the Hot Springs Family YMCA.

Fontaine reminds me of the prophet Amos, for Amos was neither a prophet nor the son of a prophet. He was but a herdsman and gatherer of sycamore fruit. A common man! Yet God raised Amos up with a message for the king of Israel that has never been equaled. His "prepare to meet thy God" theme has since led millions of people out of spiritual darkness.

Charles Fontaine is a man in the same tradition as Amos – a refreshingly common man of unpretentious credentials. Ironically, he was raised in Hot Springs, the birthplace of the Assemblies of God. And for forty-five years he was a member of Assemblies of God churches. He was an active deacon in his local Assemblies of God church. His lovely wife, Lynda, was raised a Southern Baptist, but for thirty years attended Assemblies of God churches. Neither are strangers or outsiders to this prestigious denomination.

In 1984, with no disagreement over doctrinal positions and no ax to grind, Charles and Lynda became members of an independent fellowship.

If there are gifts of perception and perspective, I would think Charles Fontaine has them. No trial lawyer could have followed such a trail of evidence more methodically.

In *Jimmy Swaggart: To Obey God Rather Than Men,* the author does three important things. First, he skillfully untangles a large denomination's confusing "line of authority." Since secrecy is the essence of power, then control is the intent of abused authority.

Secondly, he scripturally uncovers an erroneous process. For the bewildered clergy and laity, the writer elucidates traditionally obscure biblical "due process."

Thirdly, he simply unifies the facts. Nothing is so astonishing as common sense and plain dealing.

A mature Christian will admit when he is wrong. A "becomer" reluctantly does so. However, the Lilliputian will dwell so much on how right he is, he winds up being wrong. It happens medically, scientifically, militarily, morally, and, unfortunately, denominationally.

I trust that this scrupulous work will assist in bringing some order out of an unbiblical olla podrida. Hopefully, Ben Franklin was correct when he wisely said, "After crosses and losses, men become humbler and wiser."

Paul W. Carlin, Th.D.

# PREFACE

Few subjects have the opposing viewpoints so firmly established as the subject of the discipline of Jimmy Swaggart.

One principle viewpoint holds that he should be allowed to continue preaching – that he has repented and been forgiven and that should be the end of the matter.

The other principle viewpoint is that he should be punished for his sin – that he should be removed from the pulpit for at least the one year as demanded by the Assemblies of God, if not for life.

The two viewpoints are essentially opposites. It follows, then, that if one of them is scriptural, the other cannot be, even though it is sincerely held by many people of good will.

In this analysis, we have attempted to cut through the outer perimeter of opinion and bias and arrive at the heart of the matter: what the Bible says on the subject of the discipline of a repentant minister.

The Bible must be our final authority, even if it requires us to change our minds from what we originally thought.

> *"All scripture is given by inspiration of God, and is profitable for doctrine, for reproof, for correction, for instruction in righteousness"* (II Tim. 3:16).

While researching for this book, we have become aware that among Christians there is an unwillingness to forgive. The Bible is absolutely clear that we must forgive if God is to forgive us: *"But if ye do not forgive, neither will your Father which is in heaven forgive your trespasses"* (Mark 11:26).

And yet, when policies and traditions apply punishment instead of forgiveness, they are given precedence over the Bible. As the Apostle James said: *"These things, my brethren, ought not to be so"* (James 3:10, Amp.).

> *"Let all bitterness, and wrath, and anger, and clamour, and evil speaking, be put away from you, with all malice: And be ye kind one to another, tenderhearted, forgiving one another, even as God for Christ's sake hath forgiven you"* (Eph. 4:31, 32).

Charles R. Fontaine

# INTRODUCTION: "A Personal Note"

On April 28, 1988, at about 4:00 p.m., when the Holy Spirit impressed us to write this book, I asked, "Why us, Lord? We aren't professional writers or Bible scholars."

He said:

> "I tried to get others more qualified to write it and they won't do it. I will tell you what to write about. You do it the way I tell you and I will use it. If you won't be obedient either, I will find someone else who will do it, but you will miss the blessing of obedience just as the others will who were disobedient.

In a similar situation, on August 8, 1988, an Assemblies of God pastor wrote Jimmy Swaggart a letter telling him of a dream he had after Swaggart had resigned. He said prior to the dream he had supported the actions of the executive presbyters and, as he put it, "even joined others in verbally shredding you."

God allowed this pastor to see Swaggart ". . . broken, sobbing, and humble before the Lord, weeping hot tears of repentance." As he watched the scene, the Lord spoke to him:

1

"I have forgiven and accepted Jimmy Swaggart. He is still
My servant, and I still have a great work for him to do. I have
forgiven him and anointed him, so keep your hands off!"

He didn't give the date of the dream, but from other
comments he made in the letter, it was apparently about the
same time we were told to write this. A number of other
people have written Swaggart with similar words of encour-
agement. God is obviously vitally concerned about Jimmy
Swaggart's welfare.

In the analysis that follows, we have tried to be faithful to
the leading of the Holy Spirit. A number of times, when we
had reached an impasse, we prayed for direction and almost
instantly were given what to write. It is very humbling when
this happens.

This same strong leading of the Holy Spirit has happened
to me before, which strengthened our resolve to obey again
this time.

While serving as a deacon in an Assemblies of God
church, I was prepared to vote no on whether to invite a
certain applicant to try out for pastor. The vote of the board
had to be unanimous, so my "no" vote would have prevented
him from coming. My concern was not with him or his ministry, but had to do with a question of long-term commitment.
The Lord knew it was an honest concern.

A few hours before the vote, the Holy Spirit spoke to me
in the same way as He spoke to me about this book and very
plainly told me to change my vote to yes. He said this young
man would do more for our church in a short time than some
others could do in a lifetime. That is exactly what has happened. He is doing an excellent job as pastor. I am thankful
I was obedient then, just as we are being obedient now.

We are aware of the reaction that may result from our statement that the Holy Spirit told us what to write about. Some will reject it outright. Some will accept the possibility because He has spoken to them in a similar way.

We simply ask that you read this with an open mind and a prayerful attitude and reserve judgment until you finish. We believe the Holy Spirit will then confirm to you the truth of what we have written.

Charles R. Fontaine

# A REVIEW OF EVENTS

All of our comments are based on the assumption that Jimmy Swaggart has truly repented, asked God to forgive him, and is no longer sinning. We firmly believe this to be true because Jimmy Swaggart said it is, the fruits of his ministry indicate it is, and the Holy Spirit told us to write this.

There is no need to go into the specifics of Jimmy Swaggart's sin, even to the little we know about it. Whatever he did has been forgiven. Anyone reading this has probably read and heard the same things we have, anyway.

What we want to look at here are the events that transpired after he was confronted with his sin. Incidentally, there are few, if any, examples in the Bible of anyone voluntarily coming forward and confessing that he sinned. They seemingly had to be confronted first. David, *"a man after God's own heart,"* is a prime example of this reluctancy to admit to sin. Nathan the prophet had to confront him with his sin with Bathsheba before he confessed to it.

After Swaggart was confronted, we believe that is when he did as the prodigal son: *"And when he came to himself,"* he truly repented and God forgave him.

5

On February 18, 1988, Jimmy Swaggart flew to Springfield, Missouri, the national headquarters of the Assemblies of God, his denomination, met with members of the Executive Presbytery, and confessed to moral failure.

On February 21, 1988, he went before his congregation at Family Worship Center in Baton Rouge, Louisiana, and again confessed to moral failure and asked for forgiveness of those present and those in the television audience.

He said he was stepping down from the pulpit for an "undetermined, indeterminate period of time," but said the Ministry would continue. He agreed to submit to the authority of the brethren of the Louisiana District.

In confessing to man, he followed the biblical pattern:

> *"Confess to one another therefore your faults – your slips, your false steps, your offenses, your sins; and pray [also] for one another, that you may be healed and restored – to a spiritual tone of mind and heart"* (James 5:16, Amp.).

The Louisiana District officials met and decided that among other things, he should be out of the pulpit for three months. He accepted that. However, the Executive Presbytery in Springfield said that violated the precedent established in similar circumstances within the denomination and they overrode the Louisiana decision.

Following a series of meetings and decisions that extended over several weeks, conditions were imposed on him by the Executive Presbytery that almost certainly would have destroyed the worldwide ministry for which he is responsible. He refused the conditions and resigned as a minister from the Assemblies of God. On April 8, 1988, the denomination dismissed Jimmy Swaggart. He said he would still honor his commitment to stay out of the pulpit for three months, and he did so.

He returned to the pulpit on May 22, 1988, and has resumed his full schedule of ministry.

# A FOUNDATIONAL PRINCIPLE

One principle, in particular, needs to be established before we start our analysis because it is the key for everything else that follows. The one fact that determines whether or not a church can scripturally exercise discipline over a member who has fallen is: Is he repentant?

If he is repentant, the church has no authority to discipline him. If he is unrepentant, it does. Paul makes that clear in I Corinthians.

Paul has just told the church at Corinth to purge the old leaven (sin) out of their church so they will be uncontaminated. Then he writes:

> *"What [business] of mine is it and what right have I to judge outsiders? Is it not those inside [the church] upon whom you are to pass disciplinary judgment – passing censuring sentence on them [as the facts require]?"* (I Cor. 5:12, Amp.).

This establishes the principle that the local church has the scriptural authority to discipline its members. The next question is, Which members will the church pass *"censuring sentence on . . . [as the facts require]"*? And what are those facts that require *"disciplinary judgment"*? Paul tells us:

9

> *"But now I write to you not to associate with any who bears the name of [Christian] brother, if he is known to be guilty of immorality or greed, or is an idolater – that is, whose soul is devoted to any object that usurps the place of God – or [is] a person with a foul tongue (railing, abusing, reviling, slandering), or is a drunkard, or a swindler or a robber. [No] you must not so much as eat with such a person . . . Drive out that wicked one from among you – expel him from your church"* (I Cor. 5:11, 13, Amp.).

Note that Paul is telling them to remove the one who is *"known to be guilty,"* the one he calls *"that wicked one."* He is clearly describing members who were actively sinning and were unrepentant. Members who had sinned, repented, and been forgiven by God would not be described as *"wicked"* and would, therefore, not be among those he said were subject to church discipline. We can logically assume ministers were included in the instructions since Paul did not specifically exclude them.

We will identify three instances of church discipline that illustrate the principle Paul defined. The first example is of church discipline being applied to an unrepentant member and is described in I Corinthians 5. That is where the man was involved with his father's wife and Paul told them to remove him from their church. He was actively guilty of immorality.

The second example is of church discipline being applied to another unrepentant member and is described in II Corinthians 2. That is where the man sinned and was expelled from the church. He later repented and Paul told them to reinstate him.

The third example is of "church" discipline *not* being applied to a repentant disciple and is described in Luke 22. That is where Peter denied Jesus with curses, repented, and was forgiven. We will expand on this example in a later chapter.

The principle is clear. Unrepentant members are to be disciplined by expelling them from the church. If they repent, they are to be reinstated. If they are repentant before church discipline is applied, they are not to be disciplined.

# THE ASSIGNMENT

The Holy Spirit told us there are three problems we are to write about. We will cover them in three sections.

**Section 1.**
The Assemblies of God disciplinary policy: The Holy Spirit wants it changed from a punitive one to one based on love.

**Section 2.**
The criticism of Jimmy Swaggart: The Holy Spirit wants it stopped.

**Section 3.**
The financial support for Jimmy Swaggart Ministries: The Holy Spirit wants Christians to support Jimmy Swaggart Ministries.

The Holy Spirit said:

> "If the disciplinary policy is not changed, there will be a time in the not-too-distant future that the entire denomination is going to suffer because of misconduct by its national leaders.

"However, if they will base their conduct toward fallen and repentant brothers on love, they will personally benefit from the change and the denomination will be an example to the world of God's love in action."

Jesus put it this way: *"This is my commandment, That ye love one another, as I have loved you"* (John 15:12).

The warning to denominational leaders if the policy is not changed is this:

> *"Judge not, that ye be not judged. For with what judgment ye judge, ye shall be judged: and with what measure ye mete, it shall be measured to you again"* (Matt. 7:1, 2).

We will come back to this principle again later in our analysis.

Before we look into these very sensitive and volatile subjects, let us say that we believe the men who are participating in this matter at both state and national levels are trying to do what they think is right.

Unfortunately, they are making decisions and taking actions under the influence of a policy that the Holy Spirit said must be changed. Some very serious problems have developed as a result of that influence, as we shall show.

Please note that we will be analyzing only decisions and actions, not the motives behind them. The Bible tells us to look at the fruit, not the motives, because our fruit is observable by man but only God knows our motives.

# THE ASSEMBLIES OF GOD DISCIPLINARY POLICY

# THE DENOMINATION AND ITS POLICY

There are certain general characteristics of a denomination that are pertinent to our analysis. A misunderstanding of these traits has led to some of the confusion surrounding Jimmy Swaggart's discipline.

1. It is a man-made organization that is neither mandated nor defined in the Bible.

2. It is a voluntary organization – that is, a given minister does not have to belong to it. He can belong to another denomination or to no denomination at all. He can join it anytime they will accept him; and, as it specifically relates to Jimmy Swaggart, he can resign from it anytime he wishes without violating scripture by doing so.

3. Its leaders, policies, decisions, and actions are not infallible and should not be expected to be infallible.

The Assemblies of God denomination, at least through its disciplinary policy, has assumed authority for the discipline of a repentant minister that it is not scripturally authorized to exercise.

17

With these observations in mind, we will now look at the first problem of our assignment: the analysis of the disciplinary policy. We are using for our source the official minutes of the Forty-Second General Council of the Assemblies of God, held on August 6-11, 1987. They contain the most recent revised constitution and bylaws.

The disciplinary policy is several pages long and is used to define the offense and the plan of rehabilitation for the offending minister. For a list of the causes for disciplinary action, see the appendix.

Our analysis of the disciplinary policy reveals it is
1. ambiguous
2. unfair
3. punitive, and
4. unscriptural.

How could a denominational policy have all this wrong with it and still be in use? One way it can happen is that policies, in general, are developed over time in response to a perceived need. At various times, they are amended or reinterpreted to meet new perceived needs. There is usually not a complete review of the original concept because, as in the case of a religious policy, it is naturally assumed to be scripturally sound. If it is not, a whole body of rules is built on a faulty foundation. That may well account for the condition of the present policy.

The other possibility is that it was done deliberately, even though it was known to be unscriptural. We believe the first possibility is the more likely.

# AMBIGUOUS

Let's turn now to the actual policy. In Article IX, A, Section 1, we read: "The aims of discipline are . . . that those under discipline *may be brought to* repentance and restoration" (our emphasis).

According to this section of the policy, the minister is still unrepentant when he enters the program because "may be brought to" is looking to a future repentance, not one that has already taken place.

However, in Article IX, A, Section 7b, we read: "The Credentials Committee shall weigh decisions on the basis of . . . the manner and thoroughness *of his repentance*" (our emphasis).

According to this section, he has already repented and the Committee will decide the quality of his repentance in determining whether or not to offer rehabilitation. A well-written policy makes it clear to whom it applies; this policy does not. It is ambiguous. In actual application, however, it is being improperly applied to repentant ministers.

# UNFAIR

The disciplinary policy is also unfair in its application. This comes about, strangely enough, because it is made to apply the same to everyone. On the face of it, that would seem to be desirable. If it is applied the same, no one can complain he is treated differently than anyone else. The problem is that not everyone's circumstances are the same; and, therefore, the effects of the discipline, which after all is the goal, can be markedly different from one person to another.

Let's take the one-year ban from the pulpit, for example. We will ignore, for the moment, whether the ban itself is right or wrong and just look at its effect on two different ministers.

To one minister, the year out of the pulpit may be just what he needed. Maybe his failure resulted from "burnout." He is financially secure, so he can relax during the year out of the pulpit and return refreshed and ready to minister again.

To another minister, the year out of the pulpit may be disastrous for him. Let's say he is not a young man and his health is not too good. Let's also say he has pastored ever since Bible school and has never worked at any other job. Those conditions are reasonable assumptions for purposes of illustration, we believe. How does he support his family for the year he is not allowed to minister? Our guess is that it is left up to him. There is no indication the denomination helps him in any way. We see the same discipline, but two very different effects.

One mechanism used to ensure equal treatment, but not necessarily fair treatment, is precedent. We have heard precedent referred to several times concerning Jimmy Swaggart, as in: "They didn't have a choice; they had to treat him just like everyone else." We will see later how that one factor played a very big part in this whole episode.

The official statement on the dismissal was read by G. Raymond Carlson, the General Superintendent of the Assemblies of God at the time Jimmy Swaggart was dismissed. As reported in the May 15, 1988, *Pentecostal Evangel,* he said:

> "While the decisions we have had to make have been difficult, at the same time they have been predictable; predictable because the Assemblies of God has guidelines for dealing with matters such as these . . . It is on the basis of *precedent* and our own bylaws . . ." (our emphasis).

In answer to a reporter's question following Carlson's statement, Carlson emphasized that the decision to dismiss Swaggart was unanimous on the part of the thirteen members of the Executive Presbytery. We would expect that, since they were following precedent.

The very concept of following precedent in the application of this policy violates biblical principle. It precludes allowing God to do His will in each individual situation. His will has been locked out of the process by precedent.

The obvious result of allowing precedent to dictate sameness is to allow the executive presbyters to say ahead of time, in effect: "This we *will* do." James warns us about that:

*"Now listen, you who say, 'Today or tomorrow we will go to this or that city . . .' Why, you do not even know what will happen tomorrow . . . Instead, you ought to say, 'If it is the Lord's will, we will live and do this or that' "* (James 4:13-15, NIV).

That is clearly not describing the making of decisions by precedent, but, rather, implicit in the verses is that God must be free to do His will in the matter, even if His will in a present situation is different from what was done in the past. As we have seen, in matters covered by this policy, He is not free to do His will because they are dictated by precedent.

Suppose, for example, that each one of the thirteen executive presbyters had felt impressed by the Holy Spirit to accept the three-month ban from the pulpit recommended by the Louisiana district. For all we know, some may have felt that way. In any event, they could not have responded to the Holy Spirit's leading because they had locked themselves into following precedent.

Incidentally, if they *had* accepted the Louisiana district's plan, everything would be pretty much back to normal by now. His three-month ban would be over and he would still be in the Assemblies of God. Most television stations would still be carrying his programs because he would not have had to refuse the disciplinary program of Springfield, which is the reason they gave for removing him. Much of his financial support would have stayed with him or quickly returned, especially within the denomination.

As we shall show in later chapters, the Executive Presbytery actually violated the Constitution and Bylaws of the Assemblies of God when it refused to accept the district's disciplinary plan with its three-month ban from the pulpit. So in a very real sense, Jimmy Swaggart's present difficulties can be attributed to the unconstitutional conduct of the Executive Presbytery. That may be difficult to understand this early in the book, but it will get clearer as we proceed.

God treats each one of us as individuals. He is not limited in His actions by precedent. After Jesus told Peter how he (Peter) would die, Peter asked Him how John would die. *"Jesus saith unto him, If I will that he tarry till I come, what is that to thee? follow thou me"* (John 21:22).

It is presumptuous to tell God that He has to confine His will to a man-made policy and its precedents, but that is exactly what happens every time this policy is enforced.

# PUNITIVE

Punitive means "inflicting, involving, or aiming at punishment." We find a strong element of punishment with this disciplinary policy. The emphases are ours in the following quotes. In Article IX, A, Section 1, in reference to discipline, we read this: "It is to be redemptive in nature as well as *corrective*." To correct means "to *punish* (as a child) with a view to reforming or improving." The dictionary example given to show how the word corrective is used is "corrective *punishment*."

To compound the effect of punishment inherent in the policy is this: In Article IX, A, Section 9, we read ". . . and that justice can *sometimes* best be served with *mercy*." Sometimes means "at times: now and then." In other words, mercy will now and then be employed in the application of discipline. By implication, then, mercy need not be expected most of the time, which would seem to be a gross violation of the Golden Rule.

Jesus said, without any qualification, *"Be merciful, just as your Father is merciful"* (Luke 6:36, NIV), and *"Blessed are the merciful, for they will be shown mercy"* (Matt. 5:7, NIV).

25

What about Jimmy Swaggart's discipline? Was it punishment? The news media evidently thinks so because it uses the words *punishment* and *penalty* when reporting on the story. The following examples were in the Hot Springs, Arkansas, *Sentinel-Record* and are all from the Associated Press, which means that they were distributed nationwide. The emphases are ours.

Feb. 24: "The three-month ban was recommended . . . as *punishment* following Swaggart's tearful . . . ."

Feb. 27: "Many church members who called the church headquarters said they felt the *punishment* recommended . . . ."

Mar. 28: "The Executive Presbytery, headed by General Superintendent G. Raymond Carlson, apparently wanted tougher *penalties* . . . ."

Mar. 28: ". . . some say is too lenient a *punishment* . . . ."

Apr. 10: ". . . a one-year suspension from preaching, a harsher *punishment* than originally ordered . . . ."

Apr. 10: "The *punishment* was handed down . . . ."

This next example was in a column called "Assemblies Shines in Swaggart Fuss" written by Marion Stephens, a psychology professor at Southwest Missouri State University. It appeared in the May 3, 1988, *Springfield News-Leader* and was reprinted in the June 26, 1988, *Pentecostal Evangel.*

"Swaggart has decided to take his ball, bat, and gloves and start his own game rather than accept the prescribed *punishment.*"

None of these examples are direct quotes by church officials; however, they have occurred over a five-month period and continue to occur, and we have never heard of a single instance where an attempt has been made to correct the media's use of the word punishment to describe the action taken against Jimmy Swaggart. A perfect time to print a disclaimer would have been when they reprinted the afore-mentioned column by Marion Stephens in the *Pentecostal Evangel,* but they made no such disclaimer.

Evidently, the disciplinary program is actually intended to be punishment or the leadership is content to have it perceived as punishment. The fear of punishment functions as an efficient mechanism for control, so perhaps it is felt it will keep a minister from sinning if he knows he will be punished for it.

Turn back to the appendix, however, and you will see a broad range of circumstances – specifically reflected in b, c, f, g, h, j, k, and l – that do not require any sin on the part of the minister, but can still force him into the disciplinary program with its punishment. Never knowing when he may come in conflict with one of those areas and suddenly finding himself out of the pulpit must be somewhat unsettling, to say the least. We would also guess that it limits open disagreement with Springfield.

To summarize: The reporters think the discipline is punishment. Members of the Assemblies of God think it is punishment. The public at large thinks it is punishment. It is seen as punishment and its actual effect is to punish. A reasonable conclusion, then, would seem to be: It *is* punishment; and therefore, by definition it is punitive.

Remember the assignment we are discussing in this section. The Holy Spirit said that He wants the disciplinary policy changed from a punitive one to one based on love. It seems apparent that repentant ministers are not to be punished by man.

# UNSCRIPTURAL

We have seen the words "biblical perspective," "biblical principles," and even "our church has rules based on the scriptures" to justify the disciplinary program. We have seen quotes by pastors that refer to scriptures that outline the disciplinary process to be followed. We have heard numerous people refer to the biblical authority for what the Assemblies of God did and is doing to Jimmy Swaggart. As a matter of fact, the policy itself contains this reference in Article IX, A, Section 6: ". . . discipline shall be administered prayerfully and in the fear of God, *in accordance with the Scriptures*" (our emphasis).

We went to the Bible to study the body of scriptures the people had in mind when they made those statements. If, prior to reading this book, you were among those who also assumed there was biblical authority for the discipline of Jimmy Swaggart, you would have been surprised to learn there is no authority whatsoever for the church to discipline a repentant minister. There are no scriptures that support it. There are no examples that support it. There is nothing that can be used to establish a "biblical perspective" or viewpoint

29

that supports it and there is nothing that can be used to form "biblical principles of discipline" that apply to a repentant minister. They simply don't exist.

The issue is even more serious than the nonexistence of supporting scripture, however. As we established in chapter two, the Bible defines who can properly be disciplined by the church. It is not silent on the subject. This policy is unscriptural, not just nonscriptural. It actually runs counter to the Bible on the subject of discipline of a repentant minister.

As we also discussed in chapter two, the key word is repentant. Jimmy Swaggart is repentant. The Bible says, *"If we confess our sins, he is faithful and just and will forgive us our sins and purify us from all unrighteousness"* (I John 1:9, NIV). It also says, *"For I will forgive their wickedness and will remember their sins no more"* (Heb. 8:12, NIV).

When Jimmy Swaggart repented, the Bible says God forgave him, cleansed him from all his unrighteousness, then supernaturally forgot his sin. At that point, for that sin, it was over. God forgave and forgot. By definition, then, there cannot be additional punishment after forgiveness that God ordains because He has forgotten the sin. If, for example, He required a one-year ban from the pulpit following forgiveness, then obviously He would know why the ban was in effect as punishment for a specific sin a full year after His word said He had forgotten it. The same verse that tells us He will *"forgive their wickedness"* also tells us He will *"remember their sins no more."* The "forgive" does not occur now and the "forget" a year later. Both acts occur within the same time frame.

The Bible does not even hint at a ban from the pulpit. That is purely a man-made punishment. It may relate to the "issue of accountability to man" that we will look at a little later.

Additional punishment seems to also relate to the idea that somehow God's plan, forgive and forget, is too easy. Richard Champion, editor of the *Pentecostal Evangel*, writing in the June 26, 1988, issue, called it "cheap grace." He is afraid that a minister will decide that since it is so "easy" to sin and then be forgiven, he will make a habit of it. Mr. Champion should talk with Jimmy Swaggart to see if the process of true repentance is so easy and painless.

We have heard others use the term "cheap grace" in the same context. There is no such thing as "cheap grace." The two terms are mutually exclusive. Cheap means "gained with little effort," and grace means "unmerited divine assistance given man for his regeneration or sanctification." No amount of effort, little or great, can earn grace. Grace is unmerited favor from God.

Grace can be profaned, however. Profane means "to treat (something sacred) with abuse, irreverence, or contempt." When man decides that God's grace is not sufficient and that something has to be added to it, that is treating something sacred with irreverence or contempt. It profanes it. When we sin, God's grace is sufficient to restore us. It is 100 percent of all we need. *"But where sin abounded, grace did much more abound"* (Rom. 5:20b).

Now men have said, in effect, "It is too easy; someone might take advantage of it. Let us add something to it so it won't be 'cheap grace.'" So they added a two-year disciplinary program, including a one-year ban from the pulpit, to grace. Now God's grace plus man's disciplinary program is required to restore a fallen and repentant brother. That profanes grace.

The very concept of requiring something that man can provide, in addition to the grace of God, to restore a repentant minister is preaching another gospel. It is absolutely unscriptural. Significantly, nowhere in all the pages of the disciplinary policy is there a single scripture reference to support any of it.

One more point: Since grace is unmerited favor from God, He is the only one who can determine if and when someone has taken advantage of it. Man is not in any position to determine that because man sees only the external. God sees our hearts.

Telling a weak, but sincere, brother that he is taking advantage of "cheap grace" when he has to repent of the same sin more than once could very well place a stumbling block in his way that causes him to give up seeking forgiveness. What an eternal tragedy that would be.

Some do not find acceptable the concept of forgive and forget, but that is God's way and His word tells us it is to be our way. We can forgive, but can we literally forget? As a practical matter, we probably can't; but we can treat our brother in such a way that he is never reminded of his failure by our words or actions. Certainly we are not to keep reminding him for two years, as is the case with the disciplinary program. So, in effect, we *can* forgive and forget. The Bible tells us:

> *"And whenever you stand praying, if you have anything against any one, forgive him and let it drop – leave it, let it go – in order that your Father Who is in heaven may also forgive you your [own] failings and shortcomings and let them drop"* (Mark 11:25, Amp.).

A two-year disciplinary program is inconsistent with that verse.

We believe there is also a principle in Matthew that indicates God does not intend for a repentant minister to be banned from the pulpit:

> *"Watch out for false prophets. They come to you in sheep's clothing, but inwardly they are ferocious wolves. By their fruit you will recognize them. Do people pick grapes from thornbushes, or figs from thistles? Likewise every good tree bears good fruit, but a bad tree bears bad fruit. A good tree cannot bear bad fruit, and a bad tree cannot bear good fruit"* (Matt. 7:15-18, NIV).

We quoted at length here, but we need to look at the total picture. By definition, for a tree to produce either good fruit or bad fruit, it has to be functioning as a fruit tree. If somehow its function could be interrupted or banned for a year, then during that year it would be prevented from producing fruit and would simply be a shade tree. It must be allowed to produce fruit for its fruit to be recognized. That's basic.

Just as the tree must be allowed to function as a fruit tree to produce its fruit, so must a minister be allowed to function as a minister in order to produce his fruit. *"Thus, by their fruit you will recognize them"* (Matt. 7:20, NIV).

The disciplinary policy in Article IX, A, Section 9c(2) says: "In the event his ministerial activity has been terminated, the minister must become established in a local church working under the supervision of a pastor and presbyter." It is true some fruit will be produced in that situation, but any minister will confirm that it is a far different matter to be an active minister than it is to attend church as a layman. That is the fruit we need to be able to observe – the fruit produced under the stress of ministry – because it was in that position that the failure occurred.

The position of the Assemblies of God on the one-year ban from the pulpit is reflected in this quote from the article "The Highest Trust" by Kenneth D. Barney, which appeared in the May 1, 1988, *Pentecostal Evangel:*

> "Even with its compassionate purpose, however, the program does not allow immediate restoration to the former position. For the one who has failed, time will be required to rebuild confidence and trust in those to whom he wishes to minister."

We will comment on this article in more detail in a later chapter.

The implication seems to be that his congregation and others affected by his sin can only have their confidence and trust in him restored if he is out of the ministry. If anything, it is probable that the reverse is true, that their renewed confidence and trust will be put on "hold" for the year of the ban because he has no ministry with which to produce fruit. Whereas, if he is permitted to return to his pulpit, he can win back their confidence and trust much sooner as they see his ministry bearing good fruit.

The perfect example of this is Jimmy Swaggart himself. While he was off the air for three months, to most of us his observable fruit was only his written word in letters and his magazine, *The Evangelist*. With his return to the pulpit, it is obvious the anointing is on his ministry even heavier than before and he is steadily winning back the confidence and trust of his viewers who are responsive to the Holy Spirit.

# PETER: AN EXAMPLE

When a minister receives God's call to preach, it is irrevocable:

> *"For God's gifts and His call are irrevocable – He never withdraws them when once they are given, and He does not change His mind about those to whom He gives His grace or to whom He sends His call"* (Rom. 11:29, Amp.).

God obviously knew before He irrevocably called them to preach that certain ministers would have a moral failure; however, when they repent and ask God to forgive them, He does. It would be a contradiction for Him to call someone to preach, then authorize man to stop him from doing so; and God is not a God of contradictions.

If He intended for man to have the authority to ban a repentant minister from the pulpit and thereby render void the irrevocable call God placed on him, He would have given us some indication of it in the Bible. He didn't.

For man to ignore the irrevocability of God's call and ban repentant ministers from the pulpit is, it seems to us, a direct challenge to God's sovereignty.

One of the best candidates for suspension, if God had wanted someone suspended, would seem to have been Peter when he denied, with curses, even knowing Jesus. And yet a few weeks after that denial, Peter preached on the day of Pentecost and some 3,000 were saved.

An interesting thought, to put that in perspective: If Peter had been an Assemblies of God minister, he would have violated, at the very least, Article IX, A, Section 2a: "Any conduct unbecoming to a minister . . . ." He would then have been banned from the pulpit for at least a year and could not have preached that sermon. That would have thwarted the will of God, since God obviously meant for him to preach at Pentecost. It is an excellent example of where following precedent would have been against God's will in that particular case.

So we repeat, there are no scriptural grounds for man to discipline or punish a repentant brother, layman, or minister. And in one of the best examples where it could have been used, thereby establishing a "biblical principle of discipline" for man to punish a repentant minister, just the opposite occurred. A "biblical principle of nondiscipline" was established for man to not punish a repentant minister. Peter was given a unique place in biblical history with that sermon.

*"There is a way which seemeth right unto a man . . . ."* We punish our children when they do wrong, so to some it *"seemeth right"* to punish ministers when they do wrong. *". . . but the end thereof are the ways of death"* (Prov. 14:12). What seems right to us may not be. In the matter of punishing repentant ministers, it isn't. We need to be guided by what the Bible says or does not say on the subject.

> *"Not everyone who says to me, 'Lord, Lord,' will enter the kingdom of heaven, but only he who does the will of my Father who is in heaven"* (Matt. 7:21, NIV).

We believe the *"will of my Father"* concerning discipline is to treat repentant ministers the way He said: Forgive and forget, and do not add anything to His grace; it is sufficient.

# FORGIVENESS *IS* THE ISSUE

It seems so obvious that someone whom God has forgiven should not be punished by man that we wondered how this could have become denominational policy. We believe we found a clue in an article in the *Pentecostal Evangel*.

Kenneth D. Barney wrote an article from which we quoted earlier called "The Highest Trust" that appeared in the February 1988 *Advance* magazine and was reprinted in the May 1, 1988, *Pentecostal Evangel*. Both magazines are official publications of the Assemblies of God. The article first appeared in *Advance* before Jimmy Swaggart's problems were made public, but it is not clear if Barney had knowledge of them or not.

An indication that this article reflects official policy is the Editor's note preceding the article. It says in part: "While it is addressed to ministers, we felt it was important for all members of the Assemblies of God to read this article which shows why we have a high standard for ministers." The article basically deals with forgiveness, but not in a way we might expect.

In his article, Barney says, "In the case of ministerial failure, forgiveness is not the primary issue." He says that "responsibility to the high calling of the ministry" is the supreme issue. Then he mentions the "glib comments about forgiveness which ignore the larger issue of accountability to God and man . . . ." The attitude toward forgiveness seems to be summed up in his coined expression, "forgive-and-forget syndrome."

When we hear the word syndrome, we usually think of something like Ménière's Syndrome or Acquired Immune Deficiency Syndrome (AIDS); in other words, something bad. That is because a definition of syndrome is "a group of signs and symptoms that occur together and characterize a particular abnormality." We begin to see why forgiveness is seemingly held in such low esteem when we see God's plan of forgive and forget associated with a word characterized as an abnormality.

What are the ramifications of this view of forgiveness? We have already seen the logical results in the disciplinary policy and its emphasis on punishment. If forgiveness were the primary concern, there would be no thought of punishment. But when the minister has embarrassed and brought shame not only to himself, but through guilt by association to other ministers as well, then in the denomination's eyes he has violated the "larger issue of accountability to God and man" and must be held accountable for it. He must be punished.

To put the "issue of accountability" in perspective, the "issue of accountability to God" is resolved when God forgives and forgets. The "issue of accountability to man" is resolved with two years of discipline including a one-year ban from the pulpit. We can better understand why David made the choice he did when God offered him three options following his sin of numbering the fighting men of Israel. *"David said to Gad, 'I am in deep distress. Let us fall into the hands of the Lord, for his mercy is great; but do not let me fall into the hands of men'"* (II Sam. 24:14, NIV).

When repentance and forgiveness are acknowledged as the scriptural dividing line that determines whether or not man is to discipline man, then we can see that there is no justification for disciplining Jimmy Swaggart or any other repentant minister or layman.

However, when forgiveness is downgraded in importance, as it is in Kenneth Barney's article, and we remember that all members of the Assemblies of God were encouraged to read it, we begin to see how conditioning to accept punishment of repentant ministers can develop and be tolerated by the membership in general and the ministers themselves in particular.

# A POLICY BASED ON LOVE

We have shown that the policy is (1) ambiguous, because it is not clear to whom it is directed; (2) unfair in its application, because it makes no allowances for individual circumstances; (3) punitive, and the public views it as mandating punishment; and (4) unscriptural, because it not only has no basis in scripture, but actually treats repentant brothers opposite to the way they are treated in biblical examples. Fifthly, we have suggested how the policy of punishing a repentant minister may have come about – by treating lightly God's plan of forgive and forget.

These are some of the problems with the present policy. Is there an alternative without these errors? We believe there is. Obviously there are details involved, but we believe the following general description shows how it could function scripturally.

(1) Following a sinful failure, when a minister repents, God forgives him and we forgive him – no year off, no punitive conditions imposed. (2) If he does not repent, he is removed from the fellowship.

How do we know he is truly repentant? We don't for sure because only God knows his heart; but we talk with him, pray with him, and if there is no evidence to the contrary, we take him at his word.

After he has repented, it is essential that he pray and study the Bible until the Holy Spirit has renewed his mind and he knows the guilt is from Satan, not from God. It is important at this time that he have at least one godly brother to pray with him and support him. It is a severe blow to a Christian to know he has failed God, and it may take a while on his part to recover from it to where he can resume his ministry. Satan will try to convince him he is worthless, that God wants no part of a failure who would do such a thing, and that he can never again be an effective minister. We certainly don't need to help Satan by telling him the same thing.

Will some ministers fail again? Probably, but it is far better to do what the Bible says to do – forgive and forget – and have an occasional one disappoint us and fail again, than it is to punish every one unscripturally in order to prevent any second failures. As far as that goes, there is nothing inherent in the two-year disciplinary program that guarantees to prevent a second failure either.

The guiding principle is absolutely fair to everyone: Treat each person as an individual. If he repents, he is restored to his ministry. If he doesn't, he is removed from the fellowship. The responsibility for his future lies with the individual directly involved. That is consistent with the rest of the gospel as well. Our salvation is individual and personal. Our relationship with God is individual and personal. When we stand before God, it will be as an individual, and it will be personal.

Concerning his relationship with his church, whether he stays or not is decided by the local body. If he is repentant and stays with his church, the church remains a part of the denomination. If he is unrepentant and his church for some reason wants him to stay, the church is removed from the denomination the same as he is. Again the individuals directly involved, by their own decisions and actions, set their course. The denominational leadership is not placed between God and man as they are now with the present policy.

This leaves the way open for Christian love to be manifested by all concerned without being hindered by an adversarial relationship brought on by the policy, as is now the case.

# FEBRUARY 21, 1988: A BETTER WAY

What would have happened if this new policy had been in effect when Jimmy Swaggart failed? Let's take a look at the February 21, 1988, service at Family Worship Center and compare the way it was with the way it could have been.

We won't try to fully describe the service because it was televised for all to see. Briefly, for those who didn't see it, when Jimmy Swaggart faced his congregation and the television cameras in that service and repented for his sin, he was basically on his own. To borrow a phrase from the Watergate era, Jimmy Swaggart was left to "twist slowly in the wind" as far as the Executive Presbytery was concerned. That was somewhat predictable because of the adversarial relationship that typically exists between the presbyters and the offending minister.

The alternative: If you can imagine for a moment that (1) the present disciplinary policy does not exist, (2) the denomination removes from the fellowship only those ministers who are unrepentant, and (3) the basic principle guiding the Executive Presbytery in this kind of situation is the biblical principle of forgive and forget, which is based on love, the following is what could very well have occurred at that service.

47

G. Raymond Carlson, the General Superintendent of the Assemblies of God, could have been there along with many of the executive presbyters and their wives, the Louisiana District Superintendent, and the district presbyters and their wives. They could all have been on the platform with Jimmy and his family. Remember, they knew beforehand that he was repentant because he had met with them earlier in private.

As Jimmy wept and repented before the congregation and the world, via television, they could have wept with him. The superintendents and presbyters and their wives could have held him and his family in their arms and shown by their actions true love and compassion.

Brother Carlson could have encouraged the congregation and the television audience to forgive him just as God had and the presbyters had, to love him, to support him with their calls and letters, and especially to pray for him and his family.

Brother Carlson could have further reminded the audience of how God has mightily used Jimmy Swaggart to reach hundreds of millions with the gospel, how the Ministry has shared millions of dollars with Assemblies of God missionaries to feed and educate thousands of children and build scores of churches. He could have encouraged uninterrupted financial support to assure that all this would continue by reminding the audience that getting the gospel to the lost is vital and time is short.

Brother Carlson could have pledged the full support of the Executive Presbytery to pray for Jimmy, to be there if he needed them, and to offer him any help by the denomination that he might need.

People watching this would have seen true Christian love, compassion, and forgiveness in action. Scenes of the service were shown on television throughout the world. Just imagine the impact this would have had on sinners witnessing it.

*"A new commandment I give unto you, That ye love one another; as I have loved you, that ye also love one another. By this shall all men know that ye are my disciples, if ye have love one to another"* (John 13:34, 35).

We believe God would have been pleased with the service as it could have been.

# SECTION 2

# THE CRITICISM OF
# JIMMY SWAGGART

# HIS MORAL FAILURE

The second problem we will look at is the criticism of Jimmy Swaggart. It seems to be centered around two main topics: (1) his moral failure, and (2) the assumption that he is hypocritical, unrepentant, and arrogant because he refused to accept the disciplinary program mandated by the Executive Presbytery, even though he was willing to accept the program offered by the Louisiana district. He is also being criticized for apparently failing to submit to proper authority, but we will cover that in separate chapters later in the book.

We will look first at his moral failure. Jimmy Swaggart has confessed his sin to God and asked Him to forgive him. *"If we confess our sins, He is faithful and just and will forgive us our sins and purify us from all unrighteousness"* (I John 1:9, NIV).

Note that it says *all* unrighteousness. That includes whatever he did. When the tabloids invent stories about him and comedians ridicule him, remember that God has already forgiven him for his actual sin and does not remember it against him. We should not patronize evil nor let it cause us to forget or ignore God's power to forgive and restore.

> *"So if the Son liberates you – makes you free men – then you are really and unquestionably free"* (John 8:36, Amp.).

> *"For I will forgive their wickedness and will remember their sins no more"* (Heb. 8:12, NIV).

What tremendous promises these are; and they apply directly to Jimmy Swaggart, and to you and me as well!

Swaggart also confessed publicly that he sinned and asked us to forgive him. There may be a tendency to consider as optional whether or not to forgive him. It isn't. The Bible makes it clear that as part of our Christian walk, we must forgive him.

> *"Brethren, if any person is overtaken in misconduct or sin of any sort, you who are spiritual – who are responsive to and controlled by the Spirit – should set him right and restore and reinstate him, without any sense of superiority and with all gentleness, keeping an attentive eye on yourself, lest you should be tempted also"* (Gal. 6:1, Amp.).

> *"Be gentle and forbearing with one another and, if one has a difference (a grievance or complaint) against another, readily pardoning each other; even as the Lord has freely forgiven you, so must you also [forgive]"* (Col. 3:13, Amp.).

> *"But if you do not forgive, neither will your Father in heaven forgive your failings and shortcomings"* (Mark 11:26, Amp.).

Just as God forgave Jimmy Swaggart for his moral failure, so must we forgive him for his moral failure.

# HYPOCRITICAL?

First, we will look at the criticism of hypocrisy. In August 1987, Jimmy Swaggart wrote an article in *The Evangelist*, his ministry's magazine, that supported the Assemblies of God disciplinary program and specifically supported the one-year ban from the pulpit for the offending minister. Is hypocrisy the only reason he would then refuse it when it was to be applied to him? We don't think so.

Have you ever changed your mind about anything? Sure, everyone has changed his mind about a lot of things. Are we being hypocritical when we change our minds? Of course not. One of the evidences of intelligence is the ability to reason, to look at a set of facts and draw a logical conclusion.

If the facts change or our understanding of them changes, we use our reasoning ability to draw another logical conclusion that may or may not be the same as the original conclusion.

In Jimmy Swaggart's case, in 1987 he drew his original conclusion based on the facts as he saw them at that time. After having the ban applied to him personally and seeing the destructive ramifications of it, which were not necessarily obvious to him in the abstract, he drew a new logical conclusion. He had to refuse to abide by it.

We have not talked to Jimmy Swaggart about this, so we don't know if he analyzed the policy and found it unscriptural, as we have done, or if he just intuitively now knows it is wrong. In any event, his conclusion is correct. Given the new information, the destruction of his ministry, he would have been irresponsible to have accepted the ban, regardless of his original statements on the subject. In fact, he would have been more than irresponsible; he would have disobeyed God if he had accepted the ban from preaching because God called him to preach and expects him to do so.

We have heard other ministers say, while discussing Swaggart, that if they sinned as he did, they would never preach again. If they repent of that sin, they will be disobeying God if they don't return to the ministry, just as Swaggart would have disobeyed Him. God's call is irrevocable.

We believe he acted with courage and common sense in making the decision to reject the ban. Based on the evidence, we believe the charge of hypocrisy is unfounded.

# UNREPENTANT?

Next, we will look at the criticism of unrepentance. It seems to be related to the idea that he is violating scripture by refusing the disciplinary program and, therefore, must be unrepentant and still sinning as long as he refuses it.

We covered this in detail in an earlier chapter, so we will just briefly restate it here to keep it in context. The disciplinary policy is an unscriptural policy. By definition, then, he cannot be sinning by refusing to abide by an unscriptural policy. Whether or not someone is repentant is for God to determine because repentance is internal and God alone knows the heart. He told us to watch for the external evidence of an internal repentance: his fruits. The fruits we see in Jimmy Swaggart's life and ministry now are indicating to us a genuine repentance. We will offer further evidence in a later chapter to support this assumption.

Based on the evidence, we believe the criticism of unrepentance is unfounded.

# ARROGANT?

And last, we will look at the criticism of arrogance. Arrogance means "a feeling of superiority manifested in an overbearing manner or presumptuous claims." Since we were not in any position to know what he felt inside, we have no way of knowing if he was arrogant or not.

There is no question that Jimmy Swaggart's "prefailure" manner was one of supreme confidence and, as he has since admitted, too much pride. He may well have appeared arrogant. He may well have been arrogant. We don't know.

However, the present charge of arrogance relates to his conduct now, during his "postfailure" activities. We have seen absolutely no evidence of what would be perceived to be arrogance since he publicly repented on February 21, 1988. The fruits we have seen – and that is how we are to recognize his true status – are good fruits. The Bible says a bad tree cannot bear good fruit.

The following are several direct quotations of Jimmy Swaggart's since his failure that reflect his feelings and attitudes:

"I have been abased; and even though I have tried with everything that is within me to do exactly what God has wanted done all these years, I look back now and see where there was too much of Jimmy Swaggart and not enough of Jesus Christ."

"I never thought I would see the day that Jimmy Swaggart would be helpless, but today I am helpless."

"The Ministry belongs to God. It does not belong to Jimmy Swaggart."

"I have wept enough tears to swim in."

"You see, Jimmy Swaggart does not count. I am expendable. It is the gospel of Jesus Christ that is important."

"Now, more than ever before in my life, I stand before you a needy man: I need your heart, your hand, and your love. I need your prayers. And, yes, I need your help."

We don't see any evidence of arrogance in his attitude. Rather, we see reflected, *"The sacrifices of God are a broken spirit: a broken and a contrite heart, O God, thou wilt not despise"* (Psalm 51:17).

Based on the evidence, we believe the criticism of arrogance is unfounded.

# OUR CONCLUSION

We believe, based on our analysis of the disciplinary program with (1) its unscriptural basis, (2) its destructiveness to his ministry, and (3) the voluntary nature of his association with the denomination, and based on Jimmy Swaggart's own words, of which we quoted just a few, that he not only had a right to refuse the discipline demanded by the denomination, but was required to refuse it if he were to remain true to the call God placed on his life. We believe he has conducted himself properly and with true Christian humility since his forgiveness.

We believe we have shown conclusively that the continuing criticism of Jimmy Swaggart is unwarranted concerning both his moral failure and his refusal to accept the disciplinary program with its ban from the pulpit. We believe we have also shown conclusively that he is not hypocritical, unrepentant, or arrogant.

Whether we have succeeded in proving these things or not, however, the Bible says do not criticize:

> *"You shall not go up and down as a dispenser of gossip and scandal among your people"* (Lev. 19:16a, Amp.).

61

> *"The words of a talebearer are as wounds, and they go down into the innermost parts of the belly"* (Prov. 18:8).

> *"But I tell you that men will have to give account on the day of judgment for every careless word they have spoken"* (Matt. 12:36, NIV).

There are those who do not agree with everything Jimmy Swaggart says or does. There are those who don't even like Jimmy Swaggart. But regardless of their personal opinion of him, God's word says not to criticize or gossip about him . . . or anyone else.

# THE FINANCIAL SUPPORT FOR JIMMY SWAGGART MINISTRIES

# FINANCIAL SUPPORT FALTERS

The third problem we will look at is the reduced financial support for Jimmy Swaggart Ministries and the necessity for Christians to support it. As Swaggart said, "The Ministry belongs to God. It does not belong to Jimmy Swaggart."

There is no question his admission of moral failure had a severe negative impact on the level of support for the Ministry. That would be expected. We believe, however, that when the people saw he was repentant (and that should be obvious to anyone watching his programs or reading his magazine; in other words, watching his fruits) they would, by and large, have resumed their support by now. Some have resumed it, but many have not. Why is that? We believe it is because of a faulty perception of his spiritual status, which can be summarized this way: "He repented for his moral failure and we have forgiven him for that, but he is guilty of present and continuing sin by not submitting to scriptural discipline prescribed by his denomination. Every time he preaches, therefore, he just compounds his sin." You may have supported Jimmy Swaggart Ministries prior to February 21, 1988, and dropped your support because you were led to believe that description was true. If such is your case, we will show it isn't true. But first, may we offer the following for your consideration?

When God irrevocably called Jimmy Swaggart to take the gospel to the entire world using television and crusades, He also laid the call on the hearts of enough financial supporters to make it possible. It was a very effective partnership, and hundreds of thousands of souls were saved because of the obedience of both halves of that partnership.

Jimmy Swaggart's irrevocable call is still to take the gospel to the entire world using television and crusades. He has been forgiven, his heart is pure, and he is trying to be obedient and do that. However, because his original partners have been subjected to a steady stream of misinformation for an extended period of time (some of which we detail in this book), many have been persuaded to stop their support. There are no longer enough of us to meet the need; and as a result, thousands of lost people around the world are not hearing the gospel even once and are going to hell.

If you are a former supporter, won't you please resume your place in the partnership? Jimmy needs you, and the lost around the world need you.

# MISREPRESENTATION

Who has fostered the perception that Jimmy Swaggart is guilty of continuing sin? The main source is the Assemblies of God national leadership; and through them, there are many local pastors who likewise continue the myth.

The following quotations are an indication of the way the disciplinary program is linked to scripture, thereby creating the false impression it is a scriptural disciplinary program. We have emphasized key words and phrases.

In a "News Digest" article in the May 8, 1988, *Pentecostal Evangel,* G. Raymond Carlson, General Superintendent of the Assemblies of God, said, "Paramount in the considerations of the Executive Presbytery and General Presbytery was the *'biblical perspective.'* " He also explained that one of the three criteria which guided the Executive Presbytery's decisions was *"scriptural principles of discipline."*

In "Our Church Stands Tall," an editorial printed in the June 26, 1988, *Pentecostal Evangel,* Richard G. Champion, the editor, said, "I'm grateful we have leaders who make their decisions on the *principles of the Word of God,* not on personalities or programs." In the same article, he also said, "Our church has *rules, based on the scriptures,* for dealing with ministerial sin."

We will look at this next quotation in depth because it includes the only scripture verse concerning discipline we have seen in any of the official statements concerning Jimmy Swaggart.

The official statement that outlined the rehabilitation requirements of the disciplinary program for Jimmy Swggart was read by G. Raymond Carlson and was reprinted in the May 8, 1988, *Pentecostal Evangel*. In part, it reads:

> "To follow the rules of jurisprudence is never easy for any group. However, let us put this in *biblical perspective.*"

Perspective means "the capacity to view things in their true relations or relative importance." Biblical perspective, then, as it is used here, essentially means "true viewpoint of the Bible." Now let's return to the statement and see what he considers to be the true viewpoint of the Bible on the subject of discipline as it relates to Jimmy Swaggart.

> "The Bible reminds us, *'No discipline seems pleasant at the time, but painful. Later on, however, it produces a harvest of righteousness and peace for those who have been trained by it'* (Heb. 12:11, NIV)."

Is the discipline the Bible refers to here describing the denominational discipline planned for Jimmy Swaggart? No; the verse preceding this one identifies who is providing the discipline described in verse eleven. Verse ten of Hebrews 12 reads as follows:

> "*Our fathers disciplined us* for a little while as they thought best; but *God disciplines us* for our good, that we may share in his holiness" (NIV; our emphasis).

This particular verse is comparing the discipline provided by our earthly fathers to the discipline provided by God, our Heavenly Father.

Since a denomination takes the place neither of our fathers nor of God, then the verse referred to has nothing to do with the disciplinary program imposed on a repentant Jimmy Swaggart by a denomination. It is misleading to use it in support of such a program because it is being used out of context.

# WHO SHOULD WE TRUST?

How important are statements by denominational leaders in shaping public opinion? Very important! The *Pentecostal Evangel* is read by millions of people each week. These millions then influence others. Anything appearing in the *Pentecostal Evangel*, especially anything concerning Jimmy Swaggart, has the ability to shape the thinking of untold millions of people – among them a large number of supporters and former supporters of Jimmy Swaggart Ministries.

In the same editorial by Richard G. Champion in the June 26, 1988, *Pentecostal Evangel,* from which we quoted earlier, he said:

> ". . . a vast majority of our own people and of the religious
> and secular world have seen the Assemblies of God in the
> light of our standing for biblical principles . . . ."

That is why the magazine and leaders are so influential. People trust the Assemblies of God to not mislead them.

Any reasonable person who trusted the denomination to not mislead him and who therefore didn't check things out for

71

himself could rationally conclude that the disciplinary program is ordained of God and that Jimmy Swaggart is sinning by not submitting to it.

As we showed conclusively in the analysis of the policy, there is no "biblical perspective," there are no "scriptural principles of discipline," and there are no "rules based on the scriptures" that relate to the church disciplining a repentant minister.

We also find derogatory comments which shape public opinion such as the one in the May 22, 1988, *Pentecostal Evangel* quoting an editor of the *Springfield News-Leader,* Ed Goodman:

> "It's easy for quiet acts of decency to get overlooked when a Jim Bakker or Jimmy Swaggart noisily reaps the rewards of his arrogance."

Another example appeared in a letter sent to Assemblies of God ministers on April 11, 1988, by G. Raymond Carlson following Swaggart's dismissal. It was then quoted in the May 29, 1988, *Pentecostal Evangel* in an editorial by Richard G. Champion, so millions could read it: "We believe God is giving us therapeutic cleansing as a body." The letter concerned Swaggart's dismissal, and the implication that the denomination is "cleaner" as a result is unmistakable.

To allow derogatory comments like these to be made about a fellow minister is totally out of character for an official Assemblies of God magazine and should not have been allowed by the national leadership.

# THE GOLDEN RULE

We will ask a rhetorical question at this point. If the roles were reversed and Jimmy Swaggart were shaping public opinion against the Assemblies of God by referring to non-existent scriptures, using scripture out of context, printing derogatory comments, and using the power of a worldwide magazine to cause their families and ministries to suffer great personal and financial hardship, would General Superintendent G. Raymond Carlson, the other executive presbyters, and Richard G. Champion, the editor of the *Pentecostal Evangel*, want him to stop and then to correct the damage done to them? We can be sure they would. No one, unless he has severe mental problems, enjoys being the recipient of such an onslaught.

The Golden Rule says, *"And as ye would that men should do to you, do ye also to them likewise"* (Luke 6:31). Note that it is the Golden Rule, not the Golden Suggestion. It is a command. Those are Jesus' own words. If we disobey a direct command of Jesus, we commit sin. The men we just identified fall directly under this command.

They have told the world that the disciplinary program is scriptural and, by implication, that it properly applies to repentant ministers. As we have shown, it is not and does not. In addition, they have allowed derogatory statements to appear in the *Pentecostal Evangel* that have further shaped negative opinions. Efforts are under way to remove him or keep him from virtually every television station in the country because of his refusal to accept the Assemblies of God disciplinary program. In other words, the misconception of the validity of the disciplinary program resulting from these actions by the national leaders of the denomination is having a direct, negative impact on Jimmy Swaggart's ability to continue and expand the Ministry, and thousands of souls are not being saved as a direct result.

Another real tragedy in all this misconception is that Jimmy Swaggart should be seen as an example of God's power and grace to forgive and to restore us when we fall. Instead, because of these improper actions by others, he is being used as an example of one who falls and refuses to do what is necessary to be restored.

The Golden Rule says the Assemblies of God are to correct the damage they have caused to the fullest extent they can because that is what they would want Jimmy Swaggart to do if the roles were reversed. It is not an option if they are to obey God.

# THE GOLDEN RULE IN ACTION

The following is a list of some of the actions that we believe must be taken immediately by the national leadership, unless they are going to ignore the Golden Rule. Note: All these actions must be accomplished publicly with as much publicity as possible because the object, in addition to obeying God's word, is to correct the damage done to him by the massive original negative publicity caused by the misrepresentation.

(1) Apologize to Jimmy Swaggart and his family and ask for their forgiveness.

(2) Admit the disciplinary program is not based on scripture and that Jimmy Swaggart did not sin when he refused to accept it.

(3) Encourage the public to provide immediate and substantial financial support for Jimmy Swaggart Ministries so it won't fail, but will be able to return to worldwide effectiveness.

(4) Write an editorial (Richard G. Champion's responsibility) explaining to the membership of the Assemblies of

God, in particular, the full correction story. Encourage the membership to renew its financial support of Jimmy Swaggart Ministries.

(5) Write letters directly to all media representatives who carried or are carrying his television programs and explain what happened. Specifically, let them know he did not sin when he refused the disciplinary program and encourage them to reinstate or retain his programs.

(6) Allow any Assemblies of God minister who goes to work with Jimmy Swaggart Ministries to retain his credentials, and restore any credentials that have been lifted if the ministers wish to have them restored.

(7) On a broader scale, contact all ministers who have been removed for refusal to accept the disciplinary program. If they are repentant and wish to be in the denomination again, reinstate them.

These are the minimum steps that need to be taken to help rectify the wrong that has been done to an innocent brother. Remember that when all this was done to him, God had already forgiven and forgotten Jimmy Swaggart's sin. That may be hard for some to accept, but it is straight out of the Bible. If there is a problem with accepting it, then the problem is with unbelief and that indicates an even bigger problem than Jimmy Swaggart had.

# TWO OPTIONS

We have shown the problems and we have outlined what we believe is the solution. At this point, the executive presbyters can take one of two options. One, they can accept the responsibility of their previous words and actions and rectify them to the best of their ability. In addition to the seven steps we suggested, the policy needs to be changed as soon as possible before anyone else is hurt by it. Or two, they can continue on their present course and refuse to take any corrective action. Obviously the first option is the best one, the scriptural one. Option two sets something else in motion. The Bible says:

> *"Judge not, that ye be not judged. For with what judgment ye judge, ye shall be judged: and with what measure ye mete, it shall be measured to you again"* (Matt. 7:1, 2).

If the executive presbyters take option two, that means the disciplinary policy is still in effect; and in an amazing fulfillment of scripture, they will be guilty of violating the very same part of the policy as Jimmy Swaggart, which is Article IX, A, Section 2a: "Any conduct unbecoming to a minister or indiscretions involving morals." And if the denomination is to be consistent – and it prides itself on that – then the national leadership will have to suffer the same discipline they had planned for him. Swaggart violated the second part: "indiscretions involving morals." They will be guilty of violating the first part: "Any conduct unbecoming to a minister."

Unbecoming means "not according with the standards appropriate to one's position." That would certainly describe their conduct if they take option two and refuse to correct the wrong they have done. That conduct would be "not according with the standards appropriate to" their positions as leaders of the major Pentecostal denomination.

Both parts of the policy carry the same punishment. And as Richard G. Champion said, the denomination will not make decisions based on "personalities or programs," so they will have to be disciplined by being subjected to a period of rehabilitation for not less than two years. They will lose their places of leadership and their right to preach for not less than one year. They will have to be under supervision during the period and will be counseled so they can be restored to some type of ministry, although according to Kenneth D. Barney in "The Highest Trust":

> "In fact, even after restoration he will probably have to settle for what he may consider a lesser ministry for a period of time. If this seems unappealing to our human nature, it simply emphasizes the awesome responsibility we assume when we accept ministerial recognition."

Actually, the executive presbyters have already violated Article IX, A, Section 2a, because of their enforcement of unscriptural discipline on Jimmy Swaggart and labeling of it as scriptural. From a practical standpoint, however, it is very unlikely anyone would bring charges against them since they were enforcing denominational policy, even though they have in excess of 250 years of ministry among them and should have known it is unscriptural.

Our guess, however, is that if the Assemblies of God leadership does not correct the situation on its own, there will be any number of people who will bring charges against them for continuing misconduct.

These men are in a very awkward position because regardless of which option they choose, it will be painful. If they admit the policy is unscriptural and eliminate or change it, that will be embarrassing in light of their previous public statements and conduct toward Swaggart. If they don't admit the policy is unscriptural and eliminate or change it, they will become victims of it.

# AT A CROSSROADS

What we have had to write in this analysis has been written with honest concern for the leaders of the denomination. We understand their dilemma and have been praying for them ever since we started writing this because they are at a crossroads. The decisions they make in response to the problems revealed can either correct some of the errors that have overtaken the Assemblies of God or set in motion the destruction of the Movement because it is clear that God is not pleased with things as they are. Remember, the Holy Spirit is the one who told us what to write about.

The Assemblies of God has a major thrust planned called the Decade of Harvest that envisions winning 5,000,000 persons to Christ in America, training 20,000 persons for the ministry, and starting 5,000 new churches in the decade of 1990 to 2000.

It is generally understood that God is cleaning up His church. It seems evident that the Assemblies of God is not ready for a decade of harvest until changes are made in the conduct of its basic operations – specifically the concept of discipline for repentant ministers as it is now practiced – and in its basic organizational relationships that have deteriorated into hierarchical rule. We will document the deterioration in later chapters.

We encourage everyone who reads this to pray for the national leaders as they decide how to respond; pray that they will yield to the Holy Spirit and do what is right. It will probably be the toughest thing they have ever had to do, something on par with Jimmy Swaggart's public confession on February 21, 1988, we would imagine. But just as God has seen Jimmy through it, He will see them through it, also, if they will humble themselves. This is His promise to us:

> *"My grace is sufficient for thee: for my strength is made perfect in weakness"* (II Cor. 12:9).

# SECTION 4

# A POTPOURRI

We have covered the three problem areas we were told by the Holy Spirit to write about. While researching and writing them, however, several issues emerged that do not necessarily fit into the flow of the material in the three areas, but still need to be addressed because of their relationship to the overall subject matter. These issues are included in random order in Section Four.

# CONSEQUENCES OF SIN

Unless God intervenes, and He usually does not, there are consequences to sin that we will suffer even after we repent and God forgives us. We might call these "natural" consequences.

To illustrate: If a man commits a sexual sin and contracts a venereal disease, everyone pretty much agrees it is a natural consequence of his sin.

However, if a man commits a sexual sin and does not contract a venereal disease, we are not justified in injecting him with the disease on the grounds that he should not get off without suffering the natural consequence that we think he should suffer. We might call this an "imposed" consequence.

The disciplinary program essentially functions as one of the vehicles for "injecting" a minister with imposed consequences. Regardless of the natural consequences of a sin allowed, or not allowed, by God, there is an additional list of imposed consequences he is "injected" with to make sure he is properly disciplined (punished).

In "The Highest Trust," Kenneth D. Barney said:

> "Human nature rebels against accepting the consequences of wrongdoing. For the minister, these consequences involve forfeiting many privileges and benefits formerly enjoyed."

One of these "consequences" he finds imposed on himself is being forced from the pulpit for a year – an action we have already shown to be unscriptural.

Other imposed consequences in Jimmy Swaggart's case include Christians shaping public opinion against him, Christian networks taking him off the air, Christians gossiping about him, Christian magazines printing derogatory statements about him, and Christian ministers preaching against him, dwelling on his sin and "forgetting" to mention his repentance and forgiveness.

Keep in mind that while all these consequences are being imposed on him, Jimmy Swaggart's sin has already been forgiven and forgotten by God. In the eyes of God, Jimmy Swaggart is innocent of any wrong. It makes us wonder what God must think when He sees some of His children mistreating one of His other children this way for no apparent reason.

# IS TIME-OUT REQUIRED?

Would a minister need to take any time out of the pulpit following his moral failure and repentance? We believe he probably would. God forgave him immediately when he truly repented, but it may take awhile for him to accept that he is forgiven and for his confidence to be restored. He would probably be ineffective during the time that restoration was taking place.

Ministers have been known to carry the guilt of forgiven sin with them for years, especially when others keep reminding them of it by their attitude toward them or by, for example, a two-year disciplinary program including a one-year ban from the pulpit. For the entire two years they are being reminded constantly of their failure, even though God forgave them long ago. That is not God's plan.

We believe the more spiritually mature the minister is, the sooner he *knows* he is truly forgiven and the sooner he will want to return to his pulpit. For one minister, it may take only a few days to reach that point; for another, it may take years; for another, there may never be recovery. But please note, the time it takes is between the minister and God and is determined by personal circumstances. It should not be mandated by a denomination using an unscriptural policy that, regardless of personal circumstances, requires a lengthy time out of the pulpit.

# CAN HE BE SCRIPTURALLY REMOVED?

Is a local church body justified in removing a pastor who sins, repents, and is forgiven by God? Or would removal of a repentant minister, such as the disciplinary policy requires, be considered punishment and therefore unscriptural?

Whatever mechanism a local church has for changing pastors in normal circumstances would be appropriate to employ to remove the described minister. He would not take on some sort of invulnerability by reason of his sin.

For their own spiritual well-being, the members must make sure they have forgiven him. But, depending on the nature of his sin, it may be wise that he minister elsewhere. Again note, however, he is not being prevented from pastoring. He can go to another church and do an outstanding job.

By the same token, if his church feels he should stay, that should be his and their decision to make. They should not be denied that choice by denominational policy.

# A GOOD REPORT

*"Moreover he must have a good report of them which are without; lest he fall into reproach and the snare of the devil"* (I Tim. 3:7).

This verse has been used to justify keeping Jimmy Swaggart out of the pulpit until he is respected by unbelievers.

The Apostle Paul suffered beatings, imprisonments, stoning, and much more by unbelievers. He did not have a good report of them. From that, we can understand that something else was evidently involved, since he would have failed his own instructions.

We believe he meant the minister was not to give the unbeliever any *legitimate* reason for a bad report. If he were held in contempt by unbelievers because he preached the gospel, but his personal life was above reproach, then that verse would obviously not apply.

Certainly Jimmy Swaggart's personal life was at least partly responsible for his bad report of unbelievers. In addition, even before his failure he had a "bad report" among many because of the uncompromising gospel he preached. It put them under conviction.

Does that mean he falls within the meaning of that verse and therefore should stay out of the pulpit until the world respects him? If they never have a good report of him, does that mean he should stay out of the pulpit the rest of his life? We don't believe that is what is intended by that verse.

We believe Paul was writing about a minister whose current life-style was causing reproach. He was not to preach as long as his life-style gave legitimate cause for reproach. For example, if Jimmy Swaggart were openly sinning and continuing to preach, he would be bringing justifiable reproach on himself and the ministry of the gospel.

When he confessed his sin and repented, God forgave him. The call to preach is irrevocable (Rom. 11:29), so God intends for him to continue preaching. His personal life is now above reproach; and for unbelievers to be able to keep him out of the pulpit on the basis of past and forgiven sin is to let unbelievers dictate to God that a given individual will not preach, when God told him to do so. It is inconceivable that God would allow unbelievers or anyone else to hold that kind of power.

Therefore, we do not believe there is any scriptural reason for Jimmy Swaggart to refrain from preaching. On the contrary, he is not justified in not preaching because God told him to do so. There will be countless millions who will be eternally grateful that he obeyed.

# NOTHING HAS CHANGED

At the National Pastors/Sunday School Convention of the Assemblies of God in Springfield, Missouri, on August 17-19, 1988, a Pastors Open Forum was held where pastors were able to question all but two of the executive presbyters on a range of topics. The Forum was open to all the pastors at the convention and 1,000 to 1,200 attended. The October 9, 1988, *Pentecostal Evangel* reported on the meeting.

The answers to questions about Jimmy Swaggart seem to indicate that, if anything, after more than four months, negative attitudes are even harder than before. They seem to be totally ignoring the good fruits of his ministry since he returned to television in May 1988. It is almost like his restoration is an embarrassment to them.

G. Raymond Carlson, the General Superintendent, repeated his explanation that the rehabilitation program which Swaggart rejected was based on "careful consideration of Scripture, precedent, and the General Council constitution and bylaws." Again we wonder which scriptures, that when "careful consideration" was given to them, yielded a two-year disciplinary program that included a one-year ban from the pulpit, but he didn't say.

Robert Schmidgall, executive presbyter from the Great Lakes area, "drew strong support from the pastors present when he spoke of Swaggart's current situation":

> "My view of this situation is that our brother (Swaggart) is guilty of blatant defiance of spiritual authority. The major problem is that a brother refused genuine spiritual help.
>
> "It is our understanding that no Assemblies of God minister should be associated with Jimmy Swaggart Ministries in a crusade or in any way."

We will comment on his entire statement because it is the best example we have seen of the prejudicial attitude of the Assemblies of God toward Jimmy Swaggart.

He referred to "Swaggart's current situation." The meeting at which these comments were made took place in August 1988. Swaggart was dismissed from the Assemblies of God in April 1988, four months earlier. Therefore, his "current situation" is that they have no administrative or spiritual relationship with him at all. Indeed, if any one of them established a relationship, he would lose his credentials. That is significant in light of the next comment Schmidgall made: ". . . our brother (Swaggart) is guilty of blatant defiance of spiritual authority."

First a comment on the timing. If he had said, ". . . our brother (Swaggart) *was* guilty of blatant defiance of spiritual authority," we could have understood that he was referring to the time leading up to Swaggart's dismissal. When he used the word "is" instead" of "was" and linked it to "Swaggart's current situation," it implies he is continuing to "defy spiritual authority" (sinning) right up to the present (August 1988).

From the point of Swaggart's dismissal in April 1988, the Assemblies of God has provided no more "spiritual authority" for him to "defy" than any other denomination has provided. They simply have no connection with him, by their own wishes. To imply they still exercise spiritual authority over him and that he is unscripturally defying it is to continue the misrepresentation of his spiritual status, which we covered in detail in a previous chapter.

Second, to use the term "blatant defiance" to describe his present or past conduct is typical of the derogatory comments we reviewed earlier that have continued to contribute to the negative attitudes toward Swaggart.

We will define *blatant defiance* to show just how derogatory the characterization is. Blatant means "noisy, especially in a vulgar or offensive manner: clamorous" and "completely obvious, conspicuous, or obtrusive, especially in a crass or offensive manner." Defiance means "the act or an instance of defying: challenge" and "dispositon to resist or contempt of opposition." Some of the more indicative words in the definitions are noisy, vulgar, offensive, clamorous, obtrusive, crass, challenge, resist, and contempt. The words *blatant defiance* will accurately describe the conduct of radicals in the streets shouting obscenities at police. To use those words to describe Jimmy Swaggart's conduct in this matter is, in our opinion, outside the bounds of decency.

Let's look at Swaggart's real demeanor at the beginning right on up to the present. As reported in the May 15, 1988, *Pentecostal Evangel:*

"Following the statement, Carlson responded briefly to reporters' questions. He said the executives had spoken with

> Swaggart before the statement was read and the dismissal took place. 'We shared with him' what would be done, Carlson said, and 'the conversaton was quite cordial.'"

Here is what Swaggart said in the August 1988 issue of *The Evangelist:*

> "At the outset I resolved before God, after careful deliberation and consultation with many of those around me, that I would not try to defend myself. I determined that irrespective of what was said, I would say nothing; irrespective of the accusations, I would say nothing."

Then he continued:

> "And that's what I've done. I guess that's the hardest thing I have ever done, especially realizing that people are believing lies. Everything within me wants to correct it, but the Lord said, 'Leave it in My hands.'"

In an undated letter, Swaggart said:

> "I want it perfectly understood that I hold no animosity toward those who took it out of the hands of the brethren in Louisiana."

(He is referring to the executive presbyters.)

In the September 1988 issue of *The Evangelist,* he wrote:

> "I have stood by and watched the greatest effort possibly in religious history (at least in the Pentecostal world) being lifted against us to destroy this ministry in its totality. *And I want to publicly state right now that I forgive the men who*

*have launched this effort*. I pray for them, and in the Lord we love them. We will never seek revenge, and we will never seek to bring them harm" (emphasis in the original).

To summarize: (1) Swaggart was cordial at the time of dismissal; (2) from the outset, he has refused to retaliate against his accusers; (3) he has yielded to the Lord's command: "Leave it in My hands"; (4) he publicly stated he holds no animosity toward the executive presbyters; and (5) he publicly forgave the men who are attempting to destroy his ministry.

There is quite a contrast between his public statements and the public statements of the national leadership of the Assemblies of God, isn't there? We will leave it to the reader: Do the words "blatant defiance" provide a fair description of Jimmy Swaggart's conduct?

# SPIRITUAL AUTHORITY

Aside from the derogatory nature of the statement, the main point Schmidgall was making when he said ". . . our brother (Swaggart) is guilty of blatant defiance of spiritual authority" was that Swaggart refused to submit to spiritual authority.

How does one acquire "spiritual authority"? In the Assemblies of God, the executive presbyters (and they apparently constitute the spiritual authority referred to) are elected by a two-thirds vote of the qualified voters at a General Council meeting. The meetings are held every two years.

Of the thirteen executive presbyters who participated in dismissing Jimmy Swaggart, one, the General Superintendent, did not face reelection in 1987. The other four resident presbyters who work full-time at the headquarters in Springfield, Missouri, were elected on the first ballot. Of the eight nonresident presbyters, one was elected on the first ballot, six on the second ballot, and one on the fourth ballot. None of them received a unanimous vote, and the majority of them were not elected on the first ballot. But just counting first ballot totals in each of the twelve elections, 10,476 votes were cast for 326 other candidates in the process of reelecting eleven presbyters and filling a vacancy in the twelfth office. The point we are trying to make, and please don't think we are being flippant, is that they are not serving as executive presbyters by Divine appointment. They were elected in contested elections and simply received enough votes to win.

They did not suddenly acquire spiritual authority over all pastors in the Assemblies of God by becoming executive presbyters. They can only speak with spiritual authority if they act and speak in accordance with the Bible.

If, as executive presbyters, they attempt to impose an unscriptural policy on a minister, even saying they speak as his "spiritual authority," he is not required to accede to it. Ministers are still personally responsible to God for their actions, even if those actions are mandated by church leaders. In the specific case of Jimmy Swaggart, the disciplinary program that the executive presbyters attempted to impose on him was unscriptural; he was, therefore, correct to refuse to abide by it.

Actually, because it was unscriptural, their directive to Swaggart carried no more spiritual "weight" than a similar order from a secular organization would have carried. Christians would have no problem recognizing a minister's right and, indeed, his obligation to refuse an unscriptural order from the secular organization. The principle is the same and the responsibility to refuse it is the same, regardless of the type of organization that gave the order. Unfortunately, the principle is not so easy to recognize when it is a religious body giving the unscriptural order and when it is doing so as "Spiritual Authorities."

The apostles were standing before the religious leaders of their day, also, when they had to make a decision on this very same subject.

*"And they called them, and commanded them not to speak at all nor teach in the name of Jesus. But Peter and John answered and said unto them, Whether it be right in the sight of God to hearken unto you more than unto God, judge ye. For we cannot but speak the things which we have seen and heard"* (Acts 4:18-20).

Another time in a similar setting:

*"Then Peter and the other apostles answered and said, We ought to obey God rather than men"* (Acts 5:29).

We believe everyone recognizes that the apostles made the right decision when they refused to obey the order to stop preaching. Likewise, everyone *should* recognize that Jimmy Swaggart made the right decision when he refused the order to stop preaching for the same reason as the apostles; he obeyed God rather than men.

# "GENUINE" SPIRITUAL HELP

The next part of Schmidgall's statement we will comment on is this: "The major problem is that a brother refused genuine spiritual help." That is a very peculiar thing to say, given the facts of the matter. In the April 1988 issue of *The Evangelist,* Swaggart said:

> "Under the guidance, leading, and direction of the Holy Spirit and with the help of the brethren of the Louisiana District Council of the Assemblies of God . . . this Ministry is going to go forward."

In another article in the same issue, he said:

> "When I placed myself in submission to my brethren (the Louisiana District Council of the Assemblies of God), that was the right thing to do" (parenthetic words in the original).

In addition to the counsel he received from the district brethren, which presumably ceased when he was removed from the denomination, he is currently receiving godly counsel from several of the people working with him in the Ministry. There are others, but we know Jim Rentz, co-pastor

103

of Family Worship Center; Dr. Bernard Rossier, a professor at Jimmy Swaggart Theological Seminary; Dr. Michael Haley, the president of Jimmy Swaggart Bible College; and A.R. Trotter, a highly respected name in the Assemblies of God, have been solid counselors to him. He is also blessed with his son, Donnie, and his wife, Frances, who have been solid rocks of support and counsel. The majority of these people are, or were until October 1, 1988, members of the Assemblies of God.

If they are not providing Swaggart with "genuine spiritual help," then by definition they are providing him with the opposite; their help is either genuine or not genuine. The opposite of genuine, according to Webster's, is "counterfeit and fraudulent."

Does Schmidgall really mean to imply that Swaggart has received or is receiving counterfeit and fraudulent help from these people, including Louisiana district brethren and his own wife and son? He should explain why he thinks their spiritual help is not genuine and how it differs from the spiritual help Springfield would have provided.

Why do you suppose Schmidgall would make this very serious charge? We don't know the answer to that, but something is very wrong in Springfield for it to be made because the fruits of Jimmy Swaggart's ministry clearly testify that he is getting and following godly counsel.

# A LITTLE LEAVEN

The last part of Schmidgall's statement reads as follows:

> "It is our understanding that no Assemblies of God minister should be associated with Jimmy Swaggart Ministries in a crusade or in any way."

That understanding is based on Article IX, A, Section 21 of the disciplinary policy which reads, "An improper attitude toward those dismissed from the Fellowship." "Improper attitude" is further defined in Article VIII, B, Section 10:

> "In order to render effective decisions made in the interest of proper discipline and for the protection of our assemblies, all who hold credentials shall refrain from taking any attitude toward offenders that would tend to nullify or set at naught the solemn verdict of the brethren entrusted with this responsibility."

The text is unwieldy, but it essentially describes the practice of shunning, just like the religious sect that also shuns individuals who violate various of their rules – even to wives being told to shun their husbands.

Shun means "to avoid deliberately and especially habitually." That is what credentialed ministers are ordered to do, deliberately and habitually avoid associating with dismissed ministers.

Why are we commenting on it? Because Section 21 does not legitimately apply in the Swaggart case, if indeed it applies legitimately in any case. The reason it does not apply is found in the portion of Article VIII, B, Section 10, that reads, ". . . decisions made in the interest of proper discipline." The dismissal of Jimmy Swaggart was not proper discipline. Proper means "marked by suitability, rightness, or appropriateness." It was marked by none of those.

Proper discipline would have to be scriptural discipline, and scriptural discipline can only be applied by the church to an unrepentant minister or layman. If it is applied to a repentant minister or layman, it is automatically unscriptural. Jimmy Swaggart is repentant, so the discipline applied to him was unscriptural and improper. That means the prohibition of association is also unscriptural and improper when applied to Swaggart, which then means those ministers who lost their credentials when they remained with Swaggart lost them unscripturally and improperly. Unfortunately, however, as long as Swaggart's dismissal remains in effect and the policy is not corrected, Article IX, A, Section 21 will continue to stand as a barrier to prevent any Assemblies of God minister from associating with Jimmy Swaggart Ministries, no matter how unscriptural and improper it is.

There is a lesson in I Corinthians we can apply to this. The Christians in the church at Corinth were allowing a man to remain in their fellowship who was openly sinning; he was "unscriptural." They actually boasted about his presence in their church. Paul called these people "proud and arrogant" because of it.

The national leaders of the Assemblies of God are allowing a disciplinary policy that is unscriptural to remain in its bylaws. They are proud of the policy. They have boasted about it on numerous occasions.

In the following verses, we are drawing an analogy between the "unscriptural" man being allowed to remain in the church and an unscriptural policy being allowed to remain in the bylaws. The effect is the same on the two bodies. God will not continue to bless a group that allows known sin or error to exist.

> *"It is actually reported that there is sexual immorality among you . . . And you are proud and arrogant! And you ought rather to mourn . . . until the person who has done this (shameful) thing is removed from your fellowship . . .*
>
> *"[About the condition of your church] your boasting is not good – indeed it is most unseemly and entirely out of place. Do you not know that [just] a little leaven will ferment the whole lump . . .?*
>
> *"Purge (clean out) the old leaven that you may be fresh (new) dough, still uncontaminated . . ."* (I Cor. 5:1, 2, 6, 7, Amp.).

Notice how the "leaven" of an unscriptural policy has already spread through the "lump"? At first, the unscriptural policy affected only individual ministers – in this instance, Jimmy Swaggart. Then it was extended to some ninety-two of his associates. Now every minister in the denomination is faced with the decision of what to do with the policy and the national leadership. And their decision will affect the entire membership of the Assemblies of God worldwide.

Perhaps an even more disturbing indication of the "leaven" fermenting the whole "lump" is this statement concerning the reaction of the 1,000 to 1,200 pastors in attendance:

"The executive presbyters received a standing ovation honoring them for their handling of events surrounding Swaggart."

What a sad commentary on a sad episode, that 1,000 to 1,200 pastors could have that reaction to, among other comments, the statements by Robert Schmidgall that we have just reviewed. Can the effects of the "leaven" be stopped and reversed? Short of Divine intervention, we don't know.

Here is an observation to put this in perspective. As we pointed out earlier, if Peter had been an Assemblies of God minister, he would have been on a one-year ban from the pulpit and could not have preached on the day of Pentecost. Suppose all of the early Christians had been Assemblies of God ministers. If they had continued to associate with Peter, even though he repented, they would all have lost their credentials and the church would have come to an abrupt halt. The Acts of the Apostles would have been a far different book, unless they, too, had said, "We ought to obey God rather than men."

While we are speculating, if Jesus were an executive presbyter, can you really believe He would have voted to remove Jimmy Swaggart from the Fellowship – a man whom His Father had forgiven? Can you really believe He would condone the derogatory statements by His fellow presbyters? Would He have refused to appear at Family Worship Center with Jimmy? No, everything we know of the character of Jesus tells us He would not have voted to remove him; He would not condone the derogatory statements; and He would have been at Family Worship Center on February 21, 1988, with His arms around Jimmy and his family, telling them He loves them. As a matter of fact, He was!

# SUBMISSION: TO PROPER AUTHORITY

Up to this point, our analysis of the disciplinary policy has dealt with the discipline part of it, demonstrating the fact that it is ambiguous, unfair, punitive, and, most importantly, unscriptural.

In the next several chapters we will study its implementation. We will look at the actions of the four principals involved – Jimmy Swaggart, the Louisiana District Presbytery, the General Presbytery, and the Executive Presbytery – and see if each one yielded to the proper authority.

The final and ultimate authority for establishing policy in the Assemblies of God is the General Council, which meets every two years. Its potential voting members are the ordained ministers holding current fellowship certificates, and one delegate from each Assemblies of God church that holds a Certificate of Affiliation. At the most recent General Council, held in 1987, 2,879 ordained ministers and 807 church delegates registered for the first session.

The Constitution and Bylaws reflect the policy decisions and votes of each General Council and, in effect, are the instructions to the denomination of how it is to conduct itself for the next two years until the next General Council. The

Constitution and Bylaws, then, are the written authority to which all are to submit. The General Superintendent is just as responsible to submit to its authority as is the newest minister in his first pastorate.

In earlier chapters we established that, based on the evidence, specific criticisms of Jimmy Swaggart are unfounded. The root cause for those criticisms, we believe, is the perception that he refused to submit to proper authority. If we can show conclusively that he did submit to proper authority, that should lay to rest the last grounds for concern about the legitimacy of his repentance.

Most have assumed that as it relates to the question of discipline, proper authority automatically means the Executive Presbytery. It doesn't. As we proceed, we will identify which body is the proper authority for each step in the disciplinary process, as defined by the final written authority – the Constitution and Bylaws.

For purposes of this portion of our analysis, we will treat the disciplinary policy as though it is scriptural, just as the principals did, and only concern ourselves with how it was implemented.

The tone is set for the relationship of the various entities in the Assemblies of God on the very first page of the Constitution and Bylaws. It reads in part:

> "WE BELIEVE: That we are a *cooperative fellowship* . . . whose purpose is *neither to usurp authority* over the various local assemblies, *nor to deprive them of their scriptural and local rights and privileges,* but to recognize and promote scriptural methods and order . . . and *to disapprove unscriptural methods . . . and conduct . . .*" (our emphasis).

The relationship is further defined in Constitution Article IV, *PRINCIPLES FOR FELLOWSHIP,* that reads in part:

"The Assemblies of God . . . shall recognize the *principles inherent . . . in this Fellowship, particularly the principles of unity, cooperation, and equality.* It recognizes that *these principles will enable it to achieve its priority reason-for-being . . ."* (our emphasis).

Unity, cooperation, and equality are vital elements of a healthy fellowship. Unfortunately, they are no longer as operative in the Assemblies of God as they once were. As we look at the question of submission, we will see why.

We have ranked the four principal entities in order, with the first being the most submissive to proper authority and the last being the least submissive, relative to their conduct in the Jimmy Swaggart disciplinary matter. The ranking may be a surprise to most.

1. Jimmy Swaggart: the most submissive
2. Louisiana District Presbytery
3. General Presbytery
4. Executive Presbytery: the least submissive

We will document the ranking in inverse order, beginning with the Executive Presbytery.

# SUBMISSION: EXECUTIVE PRESBYTERY

The Executive Presbytery was the least submissive of any of the principals and exhibited a disturbing disregard for the authority of the General Council and the Constitution and Bylaws.

The first example of the Executive Presbytery refusing to submit to the authority of the Constitution and Bylaws is when it withheld evidence (photographs) from the Louisiana District Presbytery.

Article IX, A, Section 3b, reads in part:

> *"Reports or complaints* against a minister, alleging violations of Assemblies of God principles (Article IX, A, Section 2) *filed with the Credentials Committee* of the General Council of the Assemblies of God, *shall be referred to the district in which the offense occurred . . ."* (our emphasis).

(The Credentials Committee mentioned above is the Executive Presbytery.)

The bylaw very clearly states that the complaint *shall* be referred to, in this instance, the Louisiana District Presbytery. Article IX, A, Section 3c, in a related matter adds "supporting instruments." As in any other document, the word *shall* does not leave an option. It is a directive to do it. The Executive Presbytery refused to submit to proper authority and did not deliver the complaint and the photographs to the Louisiana District Presbytery.

The second example of the Executive Presbytery refusing to submit to the authority of the Constitution and Bylaws is when it summoned Jimmy Swaggart to Springfield on February 18, 1988, to respond to the withheld complaint and evidence.

Article IX, A, Section 3 deals with the right of initiative; that is, which body will take the introductory step in the disciplinary process. The only time the Executive Presbytery has any authority to get involved in the initial stage is to see that a district takes action if it has failed to do so on its own.

Article IX, A, Section 3d, reads:

> "In the event the district fails to take action within 90 days after a matter has been referred to it, it shall be the responsibility of the Credentials Committee of the General Council of the Assemblies of God to see that action is initiated."

The Louisiana District Presbytery was not given the opportunity to take action because the Executive Presbytery, when it received the complaint and supporting evidence, took the initiative in the matter and started its own investigation. It did so in direct violation of the Constitution and Bylaws, which is not silent about which body does have the authority to investigate.

Article IX, A, Section 3b, reads in part:

> *"The officiary of the district* in which the alleged offense is reported to have occurred *shall be recognized as having the prior right of initiative* in matters of discipline" (our emphasis).

And we will finish the part we quoted earlier from the same bylaw:

> "Reports or complaints . . . *shall be referred to the district* in which the offense occurred *for investigation and such action as the revealed facts may warrant*" (our emphasis).

The Constitution and Bylaws is unmistakably clear that the Louisiana District Presbytery had the absolute right of initiative and the sole authority to investigate and take whatever action it felt was justified. The Executive Presbytery refused to submit to proper authority and took the initiative in the matter itself.

The third example does not involve the entire Executive Presbytery, except indirectly, but rather two of its members.

At the February 18 meeting to which it summoned Jimmy Swaggart, the Executive Presbytery pledged that what was said in the meeting would be held in strict confidence, that it would not leave the room. Any person has a right to expect that what is said between him and his lawyer, doctor, or minister will be confidential, and that is what Swaggart was led to expect. Additionally, there was no legitimate reason nor requirement to make it public.

Within the next few days, however, two of the executive presbyters, Glen D. Cole and James E. Hamill, held meetings with news media representatives and discussed elements of the confidential information in direct violation of the pledge of confidentiality. If these men had no intention of keeping the information confidential, they had a moral obligation to inform the other participants of that fact so the matter could be resolved before leaving the room. To handle it in the manner in which they did was a violation in spirit, if not in fact, of Article VII, Section 12, which reads:

"Assemblies of God ministers are encouraged to respect as sacred and confidential information confided to them while they are functioning in their ministerial capacities as spiritual counselors and are encouraged not to disclose such confidential information except with the permission of the confidant or to prevent the commission of a crime."

They were probably not functioning as his spiritual counselors in the strictest sense, so perhaps they didn't violate the letter of the Constitution and Bylaws, but that is a very fine line to draw, considering the potential for harm to a fellow minister. In any event, they gave their collective word to keep the contents of the meeting confidential and they should have kept their word.

Associated with that same meeting on February 18 in Springfield, an official spokesperson for the Executive Presbytery was quoted as saying, "Jimmy Swaggart's credentials are in danger."

Three thoughts come to mind concerning that statement. First, at that point, the Executive Presbytery was the only governing body to have talked to Swaggart, and according to the Constitution and Bylaws it does not have the authority to put his credentials in danger. Second, the statement preconditioned the public, and especially members of the Assemblies of God, to the idea that he would probably be dismissed – an unfair and unwarranted assumption at that point. And third, it placed the Louisiana District Presbytery in a position of trying to hold a fair and impartial hearing with Swaggart while other elements of the denomination had already prejudged him publicly, thereby making anything less than dismissal seem to reflect a conflict of interest or a show of favoritism on the district's part.

That statement and its timing were clearly prejudicial to Jimmy Swaggart and is another indication the Executive Presbytery refused to function within its proper role as defined by the Constitution and Bylaws.

The next example requires some background information before we discuss it. Following the February 18 meeting with the Executive Presbytery and his public confession at Family Worship Center, Swaggart met with the Louisiana District Presbytery in Alexandria and again confessed in detail and answered all their questions – for eleven hours!

There are two options available to a district presbytery when it is considering the fate of a fallen minister. It can either recommend dismissal or design a rehabilitation plan for him. If it recommends dismissal, the recommendation is to be reviewed by the Executive Presbytery, functioning as the Credentials Committee.

Article IX, A, Section 8a, reads in part:

> *"District Recommendation:* If it is determined that a *minister's credentials are to be terminated,* the district shall recommend to the Credentials Committee of the General Council of the Assemblies of God that his name be removed from the official list of ministers . . ." (our emphasis).

The Credentials Committee also has two options available to it at that point. It can either agree with the dismissal recommendation or send it back to the district presbytery for reconsideration. The authority for its actions is defined in Article IX, A, Section 8b, which reads:

> *"General Council Credentials Committee action:* The said Credentials Committee shall be authorized to comply with

the request of the district if in its judgment the district was justified in the action taken" (our note: i.e., was dismissal justified). "If the said Credentials Committee finds that justice has not been served, it may refer the case, together with its recommendations, back to the district for review and reconsideration. Disposition of the case shall await further report from the district" (our emphasis).

Note that the review process applies only when the district recommends dismissal. When it recommends rehabilitation, it is not subject to review by any other governing body. It stands as offered, to be accepted or rejected by the minister involved.

The Louisiana District Presbytery took into account the openness of Jimmy Swaggart's confession and answers to its questions, his obvious repentance and brokenness, and his willingness to submit to discipline, and designed a rehabilitation plan it felt was appropriate for him and his ministerial obligations. The presbytery was confident that its plan would restore him, not destroy him. And since according to the Constitution and Bylaws its plan was not subject to review, it publicly announced the details as the finished rehabilitation plan offered to Jimmy Swaggart.

With that background in mind, the fourth example of the Executive Presbytery refusing to submit to the authority of the Constitution and Bylaws is when it met on February 25 and 26, and following the meeting ordered the Louisiana District Presbytery to reconsider its rehabilitation plan.

The only reference in the Constitution and Bylaws to a review function by the Credentials Committee concerning discipline is in Section 8 that we just quoted that concerns dismissal. Jimmy Swaggart was not dismissed by the district, but was offered rehabilitation; therefore, the Executive Presbytery could not rightfully get involved, and by doing so it refused to submit to proper authority.

Just how knowingly the Executive Presbytery violated the Constitution and Bylaws in this particular instance is revealed by Resolution 36 that was introduced at the 1985 General Council. The resolution begins as follows:

> "WHEREAS, *it has been longstanding policy* that the *extent of ministry* an ordained minister may have while under rehabilitation must be approved by the General Council Credentials Committee; and WHEREAS, this stipulation *has not been stated in the bylaws;* therefore . . ." (our emphasis).

That reveals very clearly that the Executive Presbytery has been doing something for years that it knows was not authorized by the Constitution and Bylaws and, as the following bylaw shows, was in direct violation of what is there.

Article IX, A, Section 9c (1) reads in part:

> "The extent to which he may be permitted to minister, if any, *shall be determined by the district presbytery"* (our emphasis).

Resolution 36 adds a clause to the existing bylaw as follows.

Article IX, A, Section 9c (1) would then read in part:

> "The extent to which he may be permitted to minister, if any, shall be determined by the district presbytery, *subject to the approval of the General Council Credentials Committee"* (emphasis reflects addition made by Resolution 36).

Resolution 36, then, legalizes what has been done illegally. (It was illegal in the sense of violation of church bylaws, not the U.S. Criminal Code.) It legalizes it, that is, if it ever gets adopted by the General Council. It was introduced at the 1985 General Council, but was not adopted. It was reintroduced at the 1987 General Council and again failed to be adopted. It is scheduled to be reintroduced once again at the 1989 General Council. There is clearly not a ground swell of support to legalize the actions of the Executive Presbytery; and until they are legalized, it continues to refuse to submit to proper authority on the subject.

The next example also requires background information. Following the order by the Executive Presbytery to reconsider its decision, the Louisiana District Presbytery met again and voted to stand by its original rehabilitation plan. It has followed the Constitution and Bylaws to the letter and, therefore, had the authority for its actions. It also was convinced the plan demanded by the Executive Presbytery could literally destroy Swaggart's ministry.

The unconstitutional order by the Executive Presbytery resulted in a "constitutional crisis." On March 3, G. Raymond Carlson issued a statement announcing the Executive Presbytery had called for a special session of the General Presbytery "to make decisions regarding matters relating to Evangelist Jimmy Swaggart."

The special session was held and resulted in the fifth example of the Executive Presbytery refusing to submit to the authority of the Constitution and Bylaws. It asked for and received authority from the General Presbytery to make decisions regarding ministerial credentials. The Constitution and

Bylaws expressly gives that authority to the district presbytery when it involves the disciplinary policy. We have quoted from six bylaws in this chapter alone that reflect that authority.

During the special session, immediately following what G. Raymond Carlson said was a unanimous vote to give the Executive Presbytery the authority it requested, one of the executive presbyters stood and said the Executive Presbytery had voted at a meeting the night before to dismiss Jimmy Swaggart instead of offering him rehabilitation. They failed to mention that before the General Presbytery had voted.

That statement resulted in extensive – sometimes heated – discussion, parliamentary maneuvering, and a close vote, but the end result was that the Executive Presbytery still had the authority it had requested and it still intended to dismiss Jimmy Swaggart.

The meeting dismissed for the day, then resumed the next morning to hear the Executive Presbytery's statement announcing Jimmy Swaggart's dismissal that was to be read to the news media representatives waiting outside.

As the first order of business, an executive presbyter stood and said they had held another meeting the night before and had changed their decision from dismissal to rehabilitation. That is what was presented to the world – a compassionately worded statement in which Jimmy Swaggart was offered rehabilitation. Nothing was said about the original plan to dismiss him.

Why did we bring the description of the meeting into this analysis? Because point four of the rehabilitation plan reads, "The rehabilitation of Jimmy Swaggart shall be supervised by those persons approved by the Executive Presbytery."

We will make two points about that statement. First, how would you like to have your rehabilitation ultimately supervised by an Executive Presbytery which wanted very much to dismiss you and which probably only offered you rehabilitation because of pressure from almost half of the General Presbytery, a body to whom it is subject?

And second, that statement in the plan resulted in the sixth example of the Executive Presbytery refusing to submit to the authority of the Constitution and Bylaws because the Constitution and Bylaws assigns the responsibility to administer the rehabilitation plan to the district presbytery.

Article IX, A, Section 9c (7) reads in part:

> "The *terms of rehabilitation* as above stated *shall be administered at the discretion of the district presbytery"* (our emphasis).

The Executive Presbytery, by assuming the supervision of the rehabilitation plan, again refused to submit to proper authority.

A few days later, the seventh example of the Executive Presbytery refusing to submit to the authority of the Constitution and Bylaws occurred when it dismissed Jimmy Swaggart. The decision to dismiss a minister in a disciplinary action is also assigned to the district presbytery.

Article IX, A, Section 8a, reads in part:

> "If it is determined that a minister's credentials are to be terminated, *the district shall recommend . . . that his name be removed . . ."* (our emphasis).

There is clearly a pattern of defiance of the Constitution and Bylaws when it conflicts with an action the Executive Presbytery wishes to take, a trend that is destructive to the principles of the Fellowship.

At some point in the past, the General Council protected against a pastor's defiance of his local church's Constitution and Bylaws when it made the following a cause for disciplinary action.

Article IX, A, Section 2e, reads:

"An assumption of dictatorial authority over an assembly."

It evidently never considered the possibility of needing the protection at the national level as well.

# SUBMISSION: GENERAL PRESBYTERY

The refusal of the General Presbytery to submit to the authority of the Constitution and Bylaws is best exemplified by its failure to control the unconstitutional conduct of the Executive Presbytery.

Indeed, it not only doesn't control the unconstitutional conduct, but at times actively aids it as we saw when by unanimous vote it ignored the Constitution and Bylaws and gave the Executive Presbytery authority over Jimmy Swaggart's discipline.

The Constitution and Bylaws give the General Presbytery the necessary authority to exercise proper control over the Executive Presbytery in a general way in Constitution Article IX, Section 3, which reads in part:

> "The General Presbytery shall be the official policy-making body of the General Council when the General Council is not in session."

Its authority over the Executive Presbytery is specifically defined in Article III, Section 6h, which reads in part:

> "The Executive Presbytery shall be amenable to the General Presbytery." (Amenable means answerable.)

The General Council, meeting every two years, retains the final authority if the two bodies cannot agree on what is proper conduct for the Executive Presbytery, but in the meantime the General Presbytery's decision prevails.

Article III, Section 8a, reads in part:

> "Should an irreconcilable difference arise between the General Presbytery and the Executive Presbytery, the decision of the General Presbytery shall prevail until such time as the issue may be submitted to the General Council."

We saw an indication that such control could be effective. When the Executive Presbytery voted to change its decision on Jimmy Swaggart's future from dismissal to rehabilitation, it did so after facing opposition from less than half of the general presbyters present.

Given the authority the General Presbytery has, it must share part of the responsibility for the conduct and lack of submission to the authority of the Constitution and Bylaws exhibited by the Executive Presbytery, and all of the responsibility for its own lack of submission.

# SUBMISSION: LOUISIANA DISTRICT PRESBYTERY

The Louisiana District Presbytery submitted to the authority of the Constitution and Bylaws in its conduct except for one time. That was when it yielded to the decision of the General Presbytery which, in direct violation of the Constitution and Bylaws, had given the Executive Presbytery sole authority over Jimmy Swaggart's discipline.

To its credit, the Louisiana District Presbytery had tried very hard to follow the Constitution and Bylaws and retain the authority to discipline him, but yielded to the General Presbytery's decision rather than allow a major conflict to escalate within the denomination at that time.

We will briefly note just how solidly the conduct of the Louisiana District Presbytery rested on the Constitution and Bylaws. When the district heard Swaggart's confession on February 22, its authority for doing so is Article IX, A, Section 6, that reads in part:

> ". . . the superintendent . . . shall arrange for *a hearing by the district credentials committee* for the accused minister" (our emphasis).

His guilt was established by his confession, so the bylaw continues.

> "If the district determines that guilt has been established, *discipline shall be administered* prayerfully and in the fear of God, in accordance with the Scriptures, and *as set forth in the Constitution and Bylaws* of this ecclesiastical body" (our emphasis).

The following rather lengthy bylaw absolutely establishes the district's sole authority to discipline Jimmy Swaggart. Article IX, A, Section 9, reads in part:

> "When it has been determined, either by a *confession of the minister involved or by deliberations of the district presbytery, that there is a cause for disciplinary action* as a result of a violation of Assemblies of God principles as set forth in Article IX, A, Section 2, *it shall then be the responsibility of the district presbytery* to determine whether or not the offense warrants expulsion from the Fellowship by *dismissal* or restoration to good standing in the Fellowship through a *program of rehabilitation*" (our emphasis).

As we noted earlier, only if the district had determined to dismiss him could the Executive Presbytery or even the General Presbytery have constitutionally become involved, and then only in a review role. Otherwise, it remains solely the responsibility of the district.

Much has been said about a potential conflict of interest present in the makeup of the Louisiana District Presbytery because four of the nineteen presbyters were associated with Jimmy Swaggart Ministries, three as board members and one as co-pastor of Family Worship Center.

We believe the implication that these four men would tend toward a more lenient discipline goes back to the unscriptural concept of punishing a repentant minister. With punishment as the goal, then since they worked with Swaggart, it is assumed the four would be more lenient and would, therefore, have a conflict of interest because for a reason that has yet to be explained, it is also assumed the other fifteen presbyters would naturally want to punish him more severely.

Several thoughts come to mind at this point. The Constitution and Bylaws give the responsibility for discipline to the district presbyters, not the national presbyters. Why is that? It is because the district brethren know the fallen minister better. They will have worked closely with him in various capacities and they will likely be more sensitive to his special circumstances, if any exist. Those are all very sound reasons and they all apply to Jimmy Swaggart. All nineteen men have known him for years because he has lived and ministered in Louisiana all his adult life. It is also evident that the district brethren were more concerned with the special circumstances of his particular ministry than the national brethren seemed to be.

Conflict of interest means "a conflict between the private interests and the official responsibilities of a person in a position of trust." The private interests of the four men and the official responsibilities of all nineteen would seem to be the same – to see justice served. With no evidence to the contrary, to imply otherwise is to impugn their integrity and that enters the area of judging them, which the Bible warns us to avoid.

The fact that the Louisiana district presbyters were willing to design a rehabilitation plan that fit the situation, in spite of the pressure for harsher treatment, indicates they are men with the courage of their convictions. If the Executive Presbytery couldn't force them into a plan they felt was unjust, it is hardly likely they would allow four of their own members to do so. In any event, the district plan was adopted 19-0, which indicates a unified presbytery, not one divided 15-4 in its thinking.

The charge of favoritism in the district's handling of Swaggart's discipline is, we believe, based on a misconception of the district's responsibility.

It is generally understood that a year out of the pulpit would have destroyed Jimmy Swaggart Ministries. Three months almost destroyed it. It was with that understanding that the District Presbytery applied Article IX, A, Section 1, which reads in part:

> "The aims of discipline are that God may be honored, that the purity and *welfare of the ministry may be maintained* . . . Discipline is to be administered for the restoration of the ministry, *while fully providing for the protection of the spiritual welfare of our local assemblies"* (our emphasis).

The mention of local assemblies is an indication that the thinking behind this section envisioned only a local church needing to be protected during pastoral failure and rehabilitation. Essentially that can be accomplished by another pastor coming in and, with compassion and diplomacy, maintaining the viability of the assembly.

Maintaining the viability of Jimmy Swaggart Ministries, however, without Jimmy Swaggart being in the pulpit is extremely unlikely. In other words, like it or not, if the "welfare of the ministry (is to) be maintained," Jimmy Swaggart's rehabilitation program had to be designed specifically for him.

The Louisiana district presbyters had to know they would be charged with favoritism when they required only three months out of the pulpit; but they relied on the authority of the Constitution and Bylaws and did what had to be done to protect the Ministry, while still disciplining Jimmy Swaggart in a way they felt would restore him. They should be commended for their courage, not condemned for their supposed culpability.

# SUBMISSION:
# JIMMY SWAGGART

Jimmy Swaggart has been totally submissive to the Bible and the Constitution and Bylaws, except for one time. When the Executive Presbytery unconstitutionally summoned him to Springfield on February 18, in an effort to be submissive, he went. According to the Constitution and Bylaws, he should not have gone because, as we have already shown, the District Presbytery has the right of initiative, not the Executive Presbytery. That hardly qualifies as a criticism of being unsubmissive, however. He was just submissive to the wrong authority.

When he did appear before the Louisiana District Presbytery, he was completely cooperative. One of the district presbyters, Dr. Ansley Orfila, said this in a letter to the General Presbytery:

> "I personally was influenced by his open confession, evident repentance, and willingness to submit to his Assemblies of God brethren."

Another of the district presbyters, Jonathan E. Ziegler, said this in a letter also directed to the General Presbytery:

"Jimmy Swaggart sinned. He failed God and he failed us. I believe he has genuinely repented. And I believe God has forgiven his sin – it's under the blood.

"I am one of three counselors who meet with Jimmy Swaggart once a week and will continue to do so for two years." (Our note: the three are no longer allowed contact with Jimmy Swaggart since his dismissal, but he continues to meet with other counselors on the same basis.) "I have watched him closely. When he came to the district office to face the brethren, he told us everything there was to tell. He answered all our questions and then some. I saw a man who was broken and spent, but I also saw a man who was elated that the worst ordeal of his life was over. Now, the burden of that hidden sin was lifted and he was at peace with his God. I've watched him week after week as God is restoring him as a potter remolds a truly broken vessel. I believe Jimmy Swaggart has truly died to himself and now Jesus can live in him. He is submitting to authority and God is honoring his 'right spirit.'"

Those who charge Jimmy Swaggart with being unsubmissive have to do so in the face of the testimony of those who were directly involved with his rehabilitation. They say he is submissive.

We believe the confusion can be traced back to the statements and actions of the national leadership of the Assemblies of God in linking the disciplinary program to scripture. When he was forced to decide between accepting an unscriptural discipline or preserving the ministry God has given him, he was called unsubmissive when he chose the ministry. We covered that in detail in chapter eight.

There is another example of Jimmy Swaggart's conduct that shows us he has been submissive from the start and continues to be submissive. When he was offered the rehabilitation program by the Louisiana District Presbytery, he accepted it. Then a few weeks later he was dismissed for refusing a replacement program ordered by the Executive Presbytery. Many people probably thought he refused the second program because he decided against going through any rehabilitation at all.

He is no longer in a denomination; therefore, there is no one to force him into rehabilitation. But did you ever wonder why, since he was dismissed on April 8, he didn't return to the pulpit for another six weeks? It was because he was honoring his commitment to his brethren of the Louisiana District Presbytery to stay out of the pulpit for three months, from February 21 to May 22. You see, they are still his Christian brothers, even if they are not allowed to associate with him. He is, in fact, honoring his commitment to abide by the district's rehabilitation program in its entirety, even though he is not in any way bound to do so – except that he gave his word.

# FUNDAMENTAL PROBLEMS

It is clear that a change is taking place in the way the Assemblies of God governs itself. But it is a change that is occurring outside the constitutional framework.

We gave several examples of a total disregard for the Constitution and Bylaws by the Executive Presbytery in just one disciplinary matter. If that is an indication of general conduct, then the problem is pervasive.

Please note that we are not questioning the motives of the national leadership. The Bible is plain that we are not to do that. What we are doing is looking at its conduct and comparing that conduct with what it should be as defined by the Constitution and Bylaws. A leadership that shies away from that comparison should explain its resistance. Just as we will look at Jimmy Swaggart's fruit, we are looking at the national leadership's fruit; and it is being done with love and concern because it doesn't measure up to the standard.

Through the actions of the national leadership, the organizational structure of the Assemblies of God is gradually being changed from a fellowship in which equality, cooperation, and unity are intended to be its guiding principles toward a hierarchical denomination in which each body is subordinate to the one above it.

An Associated Press writer wrote the following in an article in the February 26, 1988, Hot Springs, Arkansas, *Sentinel-Record: "The hierarchy of the Assemblies of God* met into the night Thursday to consider toughening sanctions . . ."* (our emphasis). The writer apparently made his assumption that a hierarchy exists based on his observation of the conduct of the national leadership.

The Constitution and Bylaws were drafted to provide a fellowship, not a hierarchical denomination, and it will serve to maintain a fellowship only if all concerned will submit to its written authority.

However, when one of the governing bodies ignores the limitations placed on it by the Constitution and Bylaws and assumes authority that properly belongs elsewhere, the three principles of fellowship break down. Equality is destroyed, cooperation is demanded, and the desire for unity discourages the offended body from seeking redress.

An important principle to keep in mind by every member of the Assemblies of God, and of the news media reporting it, is that those who resist unconstitutional conduct by a governing body are not the ones who are destroying the unity of the Fellowship. That will have already been caused by the body which violated the Constitution and Bylaws in the first place. Those seeking to properly correct the violation will be trying to restore the unity of the Fellowship and need to be supported in the effort.

The General Council has to accept a major share of the responsibility for allowing the constitutional protection of the Fellowship to deteriorate in the first place. At some point in the past, the executive presbyters in office at that time took the first unconstitutional action that began the deterioration. If they had been stopped at that time, it probably would not have taken more than a comment over a cup of coffee to prevent it from happening again. They were not stopped; and if it had not been for the prominence of Jimmy Swaggart, the deterioration would possibly have continued unexposed. Unfortunately, every General Council since then has also failed to halt the deterioration, resulting in the current crisis that now has to be faced.

A Constitution and Bylaws is a living document, designed to be amended as the need arises. There are two fundamentally different ways to accomplish that.

The first way, the constitutional way, is to draft an amendment, present and defend it on its merits, and see it either rejected or adopted by the voting delegates. If it is rejected, its provisions are not implemented. If it is adopted, they are.

The other way, the unconstitutional way, is to do it the way Resolution 36 is being done. Its provisions were implemented first, in direct defiance of existing bylaws. The implementation continued until a precedent had been established. The provisions were then put into the form of a resolution, Resolution 36, and if adopted will codify the unconstitutional provisions, making them constitutional at last.

The only written argument in the resolution in favor of its adoption is, "WHEREAS, it has been longstanding policy . . . ." There is nothing in the resolution concerning any merits it may have, just its longevity, which was unconstitutionally acquired.

We discussed precedent earlier as it related to the unfairness of the disciplinary policy. Precedent is also improperly applied in the Assemblies of God to matters of constitutional order or fundamental doctrine, which is what is at issue here.

The Executive Presbytery does not have the constitutional authority to make policy, only to interpret it. In other words, the policy has to already be "on the books" before the Executive Presbytery can "legally" implement it.

Article III, Section 6b, reads in part:

> "The Executive Presbytery shall have the right and duty of *interpreting policy* originating in the legislation of the General Council or the General Presbytery" (our emphasis).

The General Presbytery, on the other hand, does have the authority to make policy decisions between General Councils; but in the area we are discussing, it must submit them to the next General Council.

Article III, Section 8a, reads in part:

> "All decisions pertaining to constitutional order or fundamental doctrines *shall be referred to the General Council for ratification* in the manner provided in the constitution" (our emphasis).

As we analyze these two bylaws, the non-role of precedent becomes clear. On the one hand, if the Executive Presbytery makes a policy decision, that in itself is unconstitutional. If it is in direct defiance of an existing bylaw, that just compounds the transgression. Time does not make an *un*constitutional action constitutional; therefore, it cannot properly acquire the status of precedent, and it is one of the functions of the General Presbytery to see that it doesn't.

On the other hand, if the General Presbytery makes a policy decision, it must be submitted to the next General Council for ratification; therefore, its maximum life is two years before it either becomes part of the Constitution and Bylaws or is rejected. Until that happens, its life is too short to qualify as a precedent. It will simply be an unratified decision of the General Presbytery. There is no justification, then, for making decisions concerning constitutional order or fundamental doctrines of the Assemblies of God on the basis of precedent.

In the future, when you see a statement like the following that was read when Jimmy Swaggart was dismissed – *"It is on the basis of precedent* and our own bylaws . . ."* – you will automatically know the Constitution and Bylaws are being circumvented (our emphasis).

# JIMMY SWAGGART

We believe we have shown conclusively that Jimmy Swaggart has been (1) the victim of an unscriptural disciplinary policy, (2) the victim of undeserved criticism, and (3) the victim of unconstitutional conduct by church leaders. His family and ministry have suffered a great deal because of these unfair actions by others.

How has Jimmy Swaggart, the man, personally handled all this? Adversity will reveal a man's basic character more quickly and more accurately than almost anything. What has it revealed about Jimmy Swaggart?

The best way we know to determine how he has come through these past few months is to compare his actual conduct with what the Bible tells us his conduct will be if he is being led by the Spirit.

> *"But the fruit of the Spirit is love, joy, peace, patience, kindness, goodness, faithfulness, gentleness and self-control. Against such things there is no law"* (Gal. 5:22, 23, NIV).

We could give our opinions of how well Jimmy Swaggart's conduct compares to the biblical standard, but a better way is to quote his own words that he has written since February 1988. We have categorized them according to the nine fruits of the Spirit.

## LOVE

Love would probably be the hardest for most of us to exhibit, especially if it involves those who misused us. He does it.

> "We believe the plan of God is that . . . we are not to defend ourselves against the statements made against us personally but are to love the individuals irrespective of what they might say or do" (July 1988, *The Evangelist*).

## JOY

Joy would likewise be pretty hard to experience during this time, but he has it.

> "I am glad I can say today that by the grace of God and through absolutely nothing I have done, there is not a single solitary thing within my life that I'm aware of that is detrimental to the great cause of Christ and the working of His Spirit within my ministry. I will ever praise the Lord for that, and I will always give Him 100 percent of the credit and the glory" (December 1988, *The Evangelist*).

## PEACE

He has undergone a real change in his life in this area. He is now more settled. He has peace.

"I have today a peace I've never known before. I used to be, in a sense, "driven" or "obsessed" with the compulsion to drive ever harder and ever faster to accomplish the Lord's wishes for this day. Well, I can now relax because I know it is *He* who sets the pace and *He* who runs the show" (October 1988, *The Evangelist,* emphasis in the original).

## PATIENCE

Patience is elusive for most of us. Someone is supposed to have said, "Lord, give me patience and I want it right now." Jimmy Swaggart's willingness to let God control the pace of his restoration tells us he has this fruit working in his life.

"As I have said many times, I do not know how God can get glory out of this tragedy; but I believe that when all is said and done, He *will* get glory. And when He does, then all the pain, the suffering, and the terrible agony that Frances, Donnie, and I have gone through will have been worth it" (August 1988, *The Evangelist,* emphasis in the original).

## KINDNESS

Our example of the fruit of kindness is what Jimmy Swaggart Ministries is doing in Africa for children.

"For the sixth year in a row, our ChildCare outreach is endeavoring to provide a meaningful and compassionate Christmas for children who are in desperate need. This year we will be helping more than 30,000 youngsters and their families in the central and southern parts of Africa" (October 1988, *The Evangelist*).

## GOODNESS

Goodness and kindness are synonyms for each other, and our examples are also similar.

"A vast majority of these people have not had meat to eat since we shipped it in last year. (They still talk excitedly about 'the day the meat came.') This year, in addition to the soybean mush we regularly provide, we will be distributing fresh, nutritious meat" (October 1988, *The Evangelist*).

## FAITHFULNESS

God wants our faithfulness and obedience. We believe He will honor Jimmy's faithfulness under stress.

"In all honesty I can say that at no time, even during the bleakest months of this depressing period, did I consider turning my back on God's calling. At no time did I consider the question of my personal future. The only question was finding the will of God and doing it" (August 1988, *The Evangelist*).

## GENTLENESS

Gentleness is not a word we usually associate with Jimmy Swaggart. Now we can.

"Because, you see, this is not the same Jimmy Swaggart writing to you as before. It's impossible for an individual to go through what Frances and I have gone through without i changing them. It has changed this preacher. By God's grace have more love, more compassion, more understanding today than before" (from an undated letter).

## SELF-CONTROL

Considering the unfairness of the attacks on Jimmy Swaggart, his self-control has to be God-given.

> "Secondly, we have been appalled at the number of ministers who have fought (with such ferocity!) to get our telecasts taken off the air. They have gone to great lengths to accomplish their goal. Yet our only defense has been to place it in the hands of the Lord" (July 1988, *The Evangelist*).

Would you agree with us that Jimmy Swaggart's life is reflecting the fruits of the Spirit? We believe that by the grace of God, his ministry is going to be more effective than ever before and more people are going to find Christ as their Saviour than ever before because he is living those fruits.

We have never met Jimmy Swaggart nor any of his family, but we would be honored to do so someday. He has become an example of what God can do with a man who will humble himself and be willing to obey, no matter what the cost.

Frances and Donnie, his wife and son, have shown their strength of character by their unfailing love and support of Jimmy when he needed them the most. That's all a man can ask from his family.

We hope you have come to love and respect Jimmy Swaggart and his family as we have. We believe they have earned it and deserve it.

# WHAT YOU CAN DO

This book has two functions: information, then action. If, having read it, you are informed but take no constructive action based on that information, it will have failed its overall purpose.

The whole reason for the book is to bring about the changes the Holy Spirit told us to write about:

1. The Assemblies of God disciplinary policy: the Holy Spirit wants it changed from a punitive one to one based on love.
2. The criticism of Jimmy Swaggart: the Holy Spirit wants it stopped.
3. The financial support for Jimmy Swaggart Ministries: the Holy Spirit wants Christians to support it.

If the Holy Spirit has spoken to your heart that the information you have read here rings true and you are willing to take constructive action to help bring about the necessary changes, here are some suggestions you might consider:

IF YOU ARE A CREDENTIALED MINISTER WHO PLANS TO BE A VOTING DELEGATE AT THE NEXT GENERAL COUNCIL, be willing to support and vote for proper corrective resolutions that may be offered. The Constitution and Bylaws were originally drafted to yield a Fellowship, and it will take courage on your part to vote to restore it to a Fellowship. At the very least, that will require the establishment of specific guidelines for the proper role of each governing body. It may also require a change of national leadership until leaders can be chosen who will be willing to work within the framework of a Fellowship with its limitation on, and diffusion of, authority.

The disciplinary policy will also need to be changed by the General Council. Please study that issue and be prepared to change it from a punitive one to one based on love – that is, forgive and forget.

You or some of your fellow ministers will have to take a leadership role in these corrective measures if they are to succeed, which may make you targets for disciplinary action under the present policy, unless enough credentialed ministers stand with you and support you.

Our goal is to get a copy of this book into the hands of virtually every pastor of an Assemblies of God church in the United States at the same time. (If you are a pastor and you received this book in the mail, you can assume we accomplished our goal.) If we can do that, perhaps a coordinated movement toward correction can result without anyone being penalized for being involved. But, in any event, please be willing to put principle above position. The future of the Fellowship may well depend on what you, personally, are willing to do.

IF YOU ARE AN EXECUTIVE PRESBYTER of the Assemblies of God, please don't consider this a personal attack on you or an attack on the denomination. It is neither.

We have written this in obedience to the Holy Spirit; therefore, how you receive it is vitally important both to you
personally and to the entire movement.

Please humble yourself the way Jimmy Swaggart humbled
himself when he was confronted and don't let pride prevent
you from supporting the necessary corrective measures concerning both the disciplinary policy and the restoration of the
Fellowship.

We are not questioning your motives in any way; please
believe that. But regardless of your motives, it is your unconstitutional conduct that has caused a crisis and you are the
best one to help repair the damage to the perception of
credibility and integrity that the Assemblies of God enjoyed
prior to this time. A very tangible way to start the restoration
is to accomplish the seven steps we suggested in Chapter 22
as soon as possible. We pray for you every morning, that you
will do the right thing.

IF YOU ARE A GENERAL PRESBYTER of the Assem-
blies of God, it is also vitally important how you receive this.
You have allowed the deterioration from a Fellowship to
hierarchical rule to occur while the General Presbytery had
the authority to prevent it. Please review past events to determine how that occurred, then be alert to prevent it from
happening again.

It is appropriate that the executive presbyters take the
steps we suggested in Chapter 22. And since the General
Presbytery unanimously, according to G. Raymond Carlson,
voted to give the Executive Presbytery unconstitutional
authority to decide Jimmy Swaggart's discipline, it would
seem to be equally appropriate if you joined them in that
corrective action.

IF YOU ARE A NEWSMAN, COMMENTATOR, OR COLUMNIST, use the information in this analysis to take action necessary to help right the injustice shown to Jimmy Swaggart. You are in a position to influence public opinion. Please use it for good.

IF YOU CONTROL PROGRAMMING at a television station that has carried or is carrying the Swaggart programs, work with him so the programs will either be reinstated or be retained on your station. Carry him financially, if necessary, until his support returns to normal. Resist the efforts to remove him from the air. Please put principle above pressure.

IF YOU ARE AN EXECUTIVE with any of the networks or cable systems that have dropped the Swaggart programs, contact him and arrange to reinstate them immediately. Carry him financially, if necessary, until his support returns to normal. Please put principle above pressure from denominational leaders who may be friends or who may even serve on your boards.

THE LAST TWO GROUPS, the program directors and network executives, will have a great deal to do with many souls being saved or lost as a direct result of their actions.

EVERYONE WHO READS THIS BOOK can personally refrain from criticizing Jimmy Swaggart, and most can support his Ministry financially. In addition, if you would like to encourage the Swaggart family with a letter or a phone call, we believe they will be very appreciative. You may contact them at

Jimmy Swaggart Ministries
P.O. Box 2550
Baton Rouge, Louisiana 70821-2550
(504) 768-8300

EVERYONE WHO READS THIS BOOK can also do what Mark Buntain, Assemblies of God missionary to India, is going to do: pray for Jimmy Swaggart. In a letter he wrote to Swaggart on March 8, 1988, he admitted he had failed Jimmy by not praying for his "life to be protected from the onslaught of Satan's power." He went on to say the following:

"I am guilty. The whole Christian community is guilty, and we need to first ask God to forgive us and then ask you to forgive us. I promise you, it will never happen again.

"Brother Jimmy, the battle is not over but neither are you and neither are we. You are God's special man, and from now on we will not only be with you but we will be behind you, behind you and around you claiming the power of Jesus' precious blood to cover and keep you.

"Please, please be encouraged. You are dearly loved" (June 1988, *The Evangelist*).

There is an example of true Christian love, compassion, and forgiveness in action. We can all take a lesson from it.

# IN CLOSING . . .

It has been difficult to write the things we have had to write about a great movement like the Assemblies of God. When the Holy Spirit directed us to write this, we had no idea we would find the things wrong that we have found.

The Assemblies of God has some impressive statistics on growth and ministry, but growth is not automatically an indication that everything is all right. The New Age Movement, for example, is growing very rapidly. The growth of the Assemblies of God will not continue unless changes are made, especially if pride is involved in the resistance of change.

A good example of how quickly circumstances can change is the sudden near-destruction of Jimmy Swaggart Ministries: One month, success; the next month, disaster! God allowed success and growth to continue even after he sinned, but only for so long. When Swaggart didn't correct it, God corrected it His way, for the whole world to see. He can do the same with denominations.

God may well have been dealing with denominational leaders a long time about the disciplinary policy. Certainly hundreds of ministers have been affected by it. It has not been corrected, so He is starting to correct it His way. His first step

155

may be to make the membership and general public aware of the error and its destructive effects by having us write this analysis. All we know for sure is the Holy Spirit said if we write this as we were told to do, He will use it. We don't know how He will use it.

If the people who can make the decisions to correct the error will open their minds to even the possibility that this is from God, He will confirm it to them and guide them in what they are to do.

If corrective action is not initiated, the Holy Spirit has already said what will happen. We recorded it at the beginning of this book, but we will repeat it here because of its seriousness.

He said:

> "If the disciplinary policy is not changed, there will be a time in the not-too-distant future that the entire denomination is going to suffer because of misconduct by its national leaders."

Then He gave this promise:

> "However, if they will base their conduct toward fallen and repentant brothers on love, they will personally benefit from the change and the denomination will be an example to the world of God's love in action."

We believe the key word is "conduct" toward fallen and repentant brothers. It is not enough to talk of compassion and concern, to say "We love you, brother." Actions have to match the words. If they can't because of a policy, the policy must be changed. At this point in time, the denomination is not an "example to the world of God's love in action." The Holy Spirit said the policy has to be changed before they can be the example God desires. There must not be anything that interferes with our ability to conduct our personal relationships or the denomination's relationships according to Jesus' instructions:

> *"And thou shalt love the Lord thy God with all thy heart, and with all thy soul, and with all thy mind, and with all thy strength: this is the first commandment. And the second is like, namely this, Thou shall love thy neighbour as thyself. There is none other commandment greater than these"* (Mark 12:30, 31).

# APPENDIX

The following is a list of violations that are among the causes for disciplinary action toward ministers of the Assemblies of God.

## Article IX, A, Section 2

a. Any conduct unbecoming to a minister or indiscretions involving morals.
b. General inefficiency in the ministry.
c. A failure or inability to represent our Pentecostal testimony correctly.
d. A contentious or noncooperative spirit.
e. An assumption of dictatorial authority over an assembly.
f. An arbitrary rejection of district counsel.
g. A declared open change in doctrinal views.
h. A habit of running into debt which brings reproach upon the cause.
i. A marriage in violation of our stand on marriage and divorce.
j. Violations of ministerial courtesy.
k. Ministry without prior approval in a non-Assemblies church.
l. An improper attitude toward those dismissed from the Fellowship.